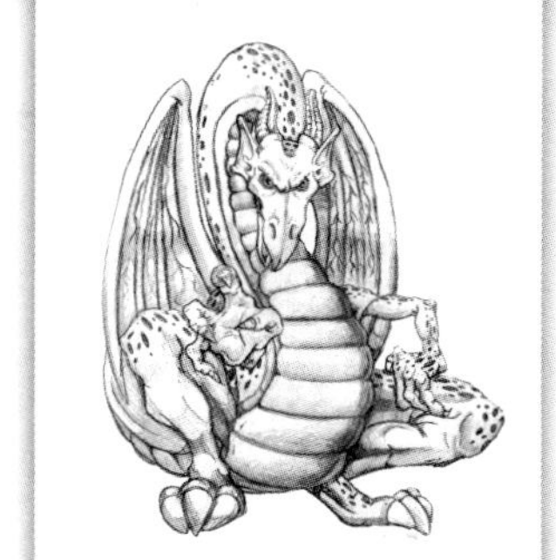

Dragons

In this book, you'll find a wealth of different types of dragons, which have been categorized using the more common terms and definitions from role-playing games, fantasy books, video games, and mythological tales. You also will discover some creatures in this book that may not appear very dragonlike (such as the naga on page 13 and the amphisbaena on page 18), but they function as dragons in certain regional mythologies. Before delving into the step-by-step lessons, you'll learn a little about my methods for drawing these fanciful creatures, including how to build on basic shapes and apply different shading techniques. And you'll learn how to get the most out of a variety of media—from charcoal pencil to India ink—so you can make your dragon drawings the best they can be. *—Michael Dobrzycki*

CONTENTS

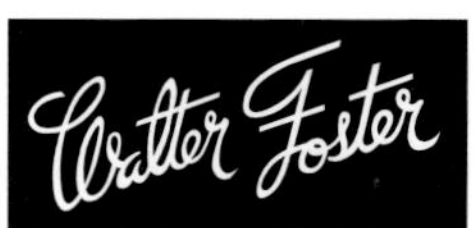

Tools and Materials

One of the great joys of drawing is that you can do it just about anywhere. There is a wide array of time-tested materials available for the amateur and professional artist alike, from pencils and papers to erasers and sharpeners. You get what you pay for, so purchase the best you can afford at the time, and upgrade your supplies whenever possible. Although anything that will make a mark can be used for some type of drawing, you'll want to make certain your magnificent efforts will last and not fade over time. And, if you want to give your dragon drawings a bit more pizazz, there are materials such as ink, charcoal, and watercolor paint that can be used to do just that. Here are some of the materials that will get you off to a good start.

▶ **Drawing Papers** For finished works of art, it's best to use single sheets of drawing paper, which are available in a range of surface textures: smooth grain *(plate finish* and *hot pressed),* medium grain *(cold pressed),* and rough to very rough. Depending on the media you use, you may want to experiment with different textures; rough paper is ideal when using charcoal, whereas smooth paper is best for ink.

▼ **Ink** To add dynamism to my artwork, I sometimes incorporate India ink, which is available in bottles. For dark, permanent lines, apply pure (undiluted) India ink with a paintbrush. I also sometimes dilute the ink with water to apply a thin, light gray tone (called a "wash"). These washes also help add depth to a drawing.

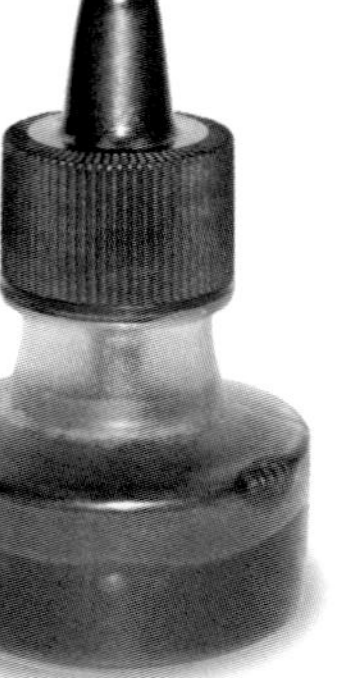

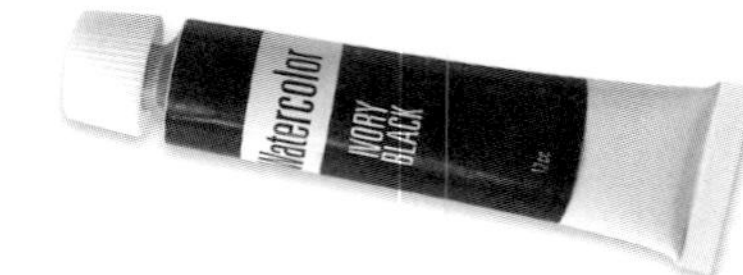

▲ **Watercolor Paint** I can achieve the same wash effect (see "Ink" at left) using watercolor paint. Watercolor paint comes in tubes or cakes; I prefer tubes.

▼ **Artist's Erasers** Different erasers serve different functions; you'll want a few different kinds on hand. You can form a kneaded eraser into small points to remove marks in tight areas. A vinyl eraser removes pencil marks thoroughly, and it serves as a workhorse for me. An art gum eraser crumbles easily, so it is less likely to mar the paper's surface—use this when doing a lot of erasing!

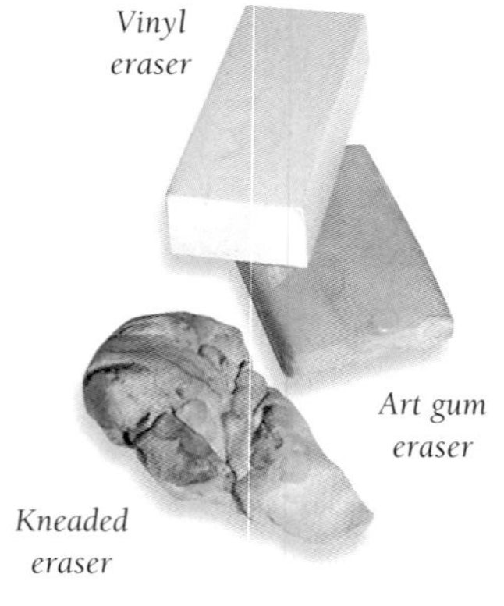

Vinyl eraser

Art gum eraser

Kneaded eraser

▼ **Color Blender** A *color blender* is a soft, rubber-tipped tool that is designed to manipulate paint on canvas. In pencil drawing, it comes in handy for making deliberate, controlled smudges.

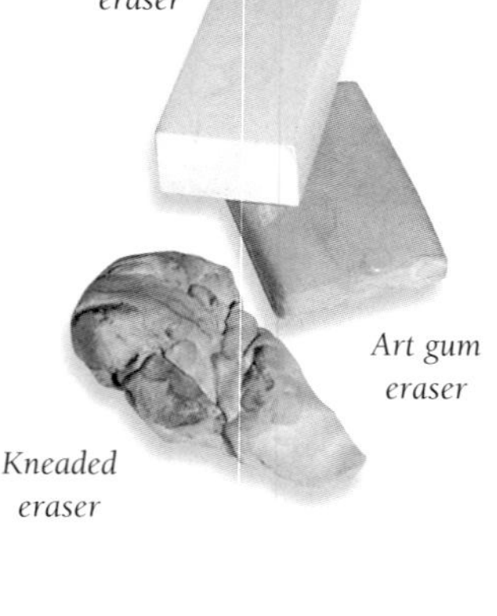

▶ **Tortillons** These paper tools (also called "blending stumps") can be used to blend and soften pencil strokes in small areas where your finger or a cloth is too large. You also can use the sides to quickly blend large areas. After use, gently rub dirty stumps on a cloth to remove excess graphite.

Drawing Tools

Drawing pencils are classified by the hardness of the lead (really graphite). The soft leads (labeled B for "black") make dense, dark marks, and the hard leads (labeled H for "hard") produce very fine, light gray lines. An HB pencil is somewhere between soft and hard. A number accompanies the letter to indicate the intensity of the lead—the higher the number, the harder or blacker the pencil. To start, purchase a minimum of three pencils: 2B, HB, and H. Aside from graphite pencil, you also can use a charcoal pencil for very dark black marks or a colored pencil for softer black marks. If you want to define your pencil lines with a bold application of ink, use waterproof ink pens or permanent marker. If you're looking for lighter, thinner lines, you even can use a regular ballpoint writing pen!

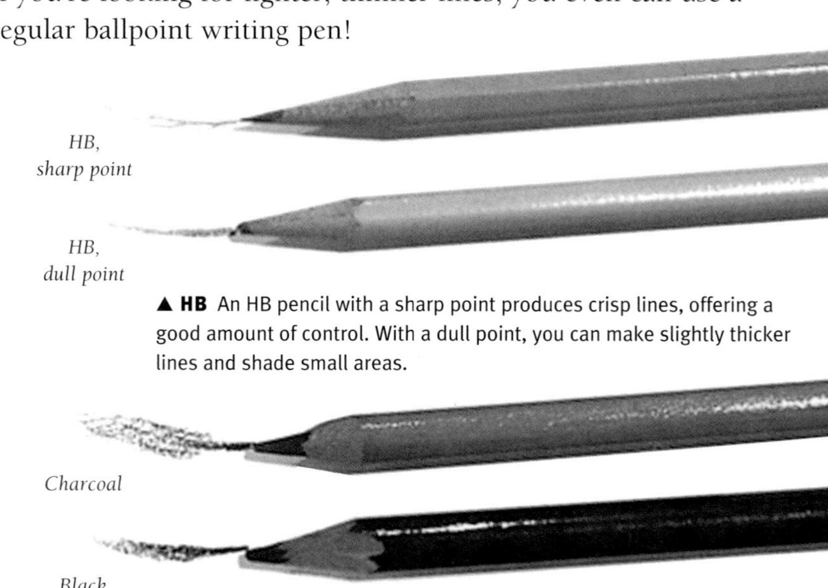

HB, sharp point

HB, dull point

▲ **HB** An HB pencil with a sharp point produces crisp lines, offering a good amount of control. With a dull point, you can make slightly thicker lines and shade small areas.

Charcoal

Black colored pencil

▲ **Charcoal and Colored Pencil** Charcoal is very soft, so it smudges easily and makes a dark mark. A black colored pencil has a waxy binder that resists smudging, to a degree—as a result, colored pencil is rather difficult to erase.

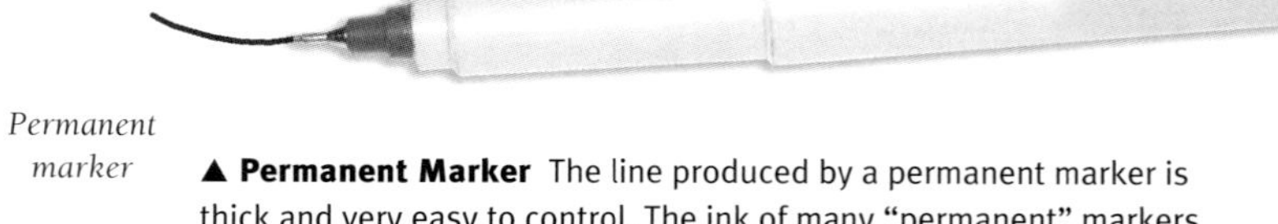

Permanent marker

▲ **Permanent Marker** The line produced by a permanent marker is thick and very easy to control. The ink of many "permanent" markers will fade over time, so you may want to spray your drawing with fixative.

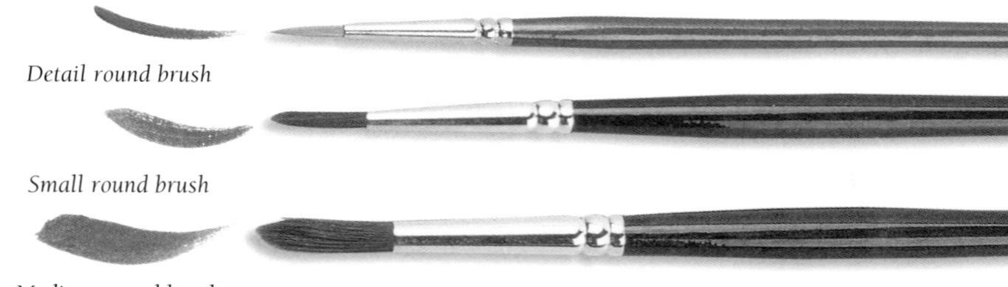

Detail round brush

Small round brush

Medium round brush

▲ **Paintbrushes** A few good paintbrushes make applying ink more enjoyable. Round brushes like these taper to a natural tip—purchase them in a variety of sizes, from very small for adding details to medium for filling in larger areas.

▶ **Waterproof Ink Pens** The thicker tips of waterproof ink pens (such as the .5 mm) are great for creating heavy lines, whereas the finer points (such as the .2 mm tip) are best for detail lines and small areas. Medium tips (such as .3 mm) offer more versatility, as you can use the side of the pen for thicker lines and the point of the pen for thinner ones.

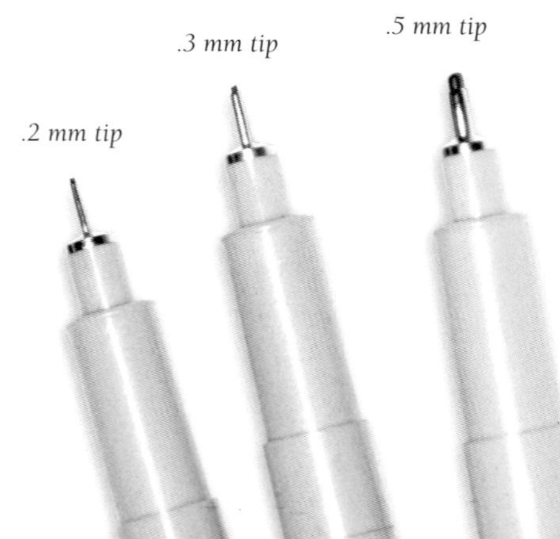

.2 mm tip

.3 mm tip

.5 mm tip

Shading Your Drawings

Once you sketch the basic shape of your subject, you can create realism and form by applying a variety of shading techniques. The information on these two pages will help you discover which methods of shading best suit your style—and you'll find that you can use the same techniques with virtually any medium, from graphite pencil to charcoal and ink. When deciding which medium to use, consider the appearance of your subject—does it have soft, fluffy hair or rough, cracked scales? Think about the textures you want to render; then refer back to these pages to see the effects you can achieve with each medium. Whichever method or medium you choose, remember to shade evenly. Instead of shading in a mechanical, side-to-side direction, use a back-and-forth motion over the same area, often changing the direction of your strokes.

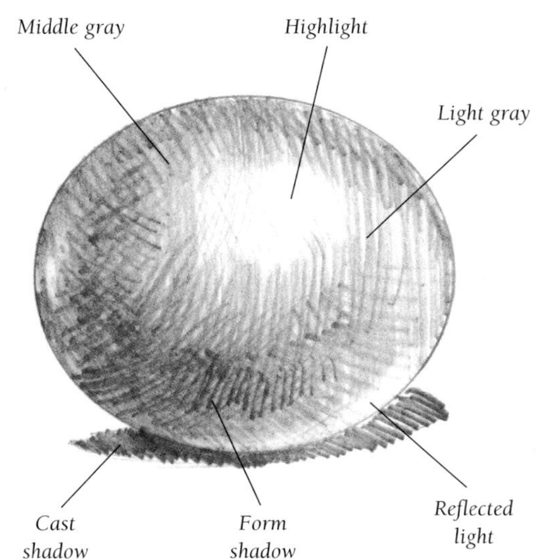

Light and Shadow The *highlight* is the lightest value, where the light source directly strikes the object. The light gray area surrounds the highlight, and the middle gray is the actual color of the egg, without any highlights or shadows. The cast shadow is the shadow that the egg casts onto the ground. The form shadow is the shadow that is on the object itself. *Reflected light* bounces up onto the object from the ground surface.

Understanding Value

Shading gives depth and form to your drawing because it creates contrasts in *value* (the relative lightness or darkness of black or a color). In pencil drawing, values range from black (the darkest value) through different shades of gray to white (the lightest value). To make a two-dimensional object appear three-dimensional, you must pay attention to the values of the highlights and shadows. Imagine the egg at upper right with no shading, just an outline. The egg would be just an oval. But by adding variations of value with light and shadow, the egg appears to have form. When shading a subject, you must always consider the light source, as this is what determines where your highlights and shadows will be. The angle, distance, and intensity of the light will affect both the shadows on an object, called "form shadows," and the shadows the object throws on other surfaces, called "cast shadows." But before you start drawing, look at a few objects around your home and study them in terms of their values. Squint your eyes, paying attention to all the lights and darks; look at the different values in the shadows cast by the objects. Then find the values you see in the value scales shown at right.

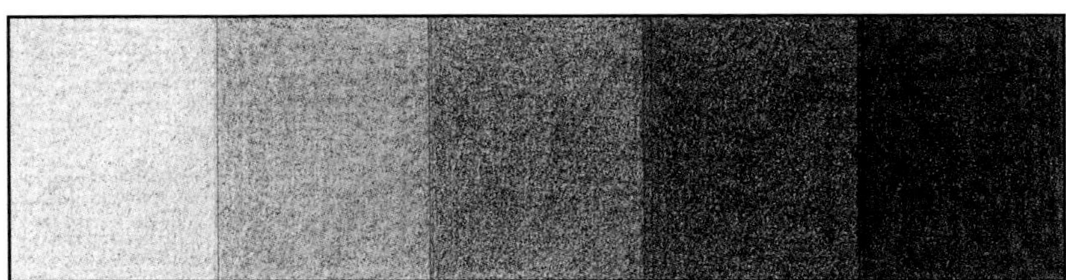

Value Scale Making your own value scale, such as the one shown above, will help familiarize you with the different variations in value. Work from light to dark, adding more and more tone for successively darker values. Different pencils produce varying value ranges; this scale was drawn with a standard HB pencil.

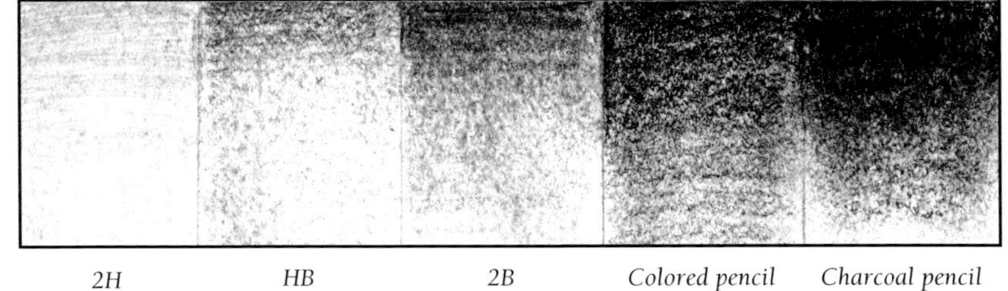

Pencil Scale As the scale above demonstrates, I can produce a range of values using different pencils. A 2H pencil creates a very light tone, whereas a charcoal pencil makes the softest, darkest tone.

Shading Styles

Artists use many different methods of shading—most build up tones from dark to light, shading the dark shadows first and then developing the entire drawing. I prefer to refine one section at a time because it helps me concentrate on the individual features—such as the head, arms, or legs. Separately attending to individual areas also keeps me from constantly moving my hand around the drawing, which helps me avoid smudging the graphite. As you can see here, I completely develop the face and most of the head before moving on to the rest of the body—and I finish shading the tail before adding the darkest darks and details such as the spots and scales.

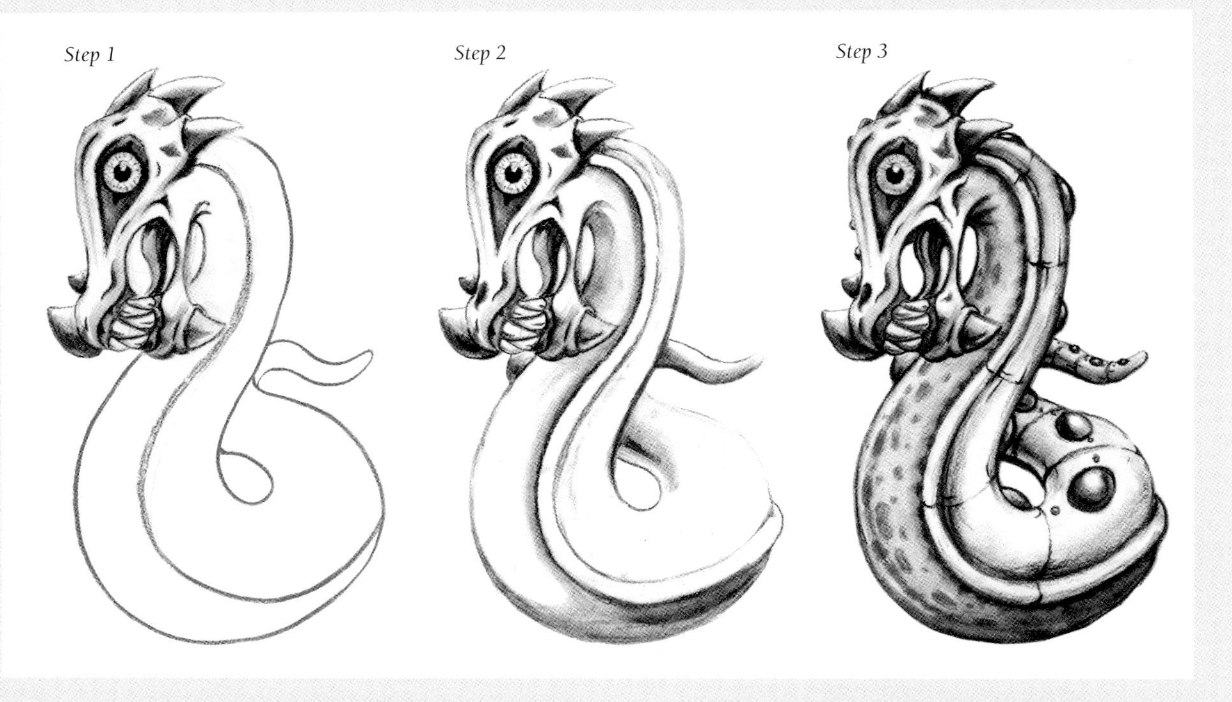

Basic Shading Techniques

By studying the basic techniques on this page, you'll be able to give your drawings a specific look or feel. The effect will vary among media, but the methods are the same. For example, shading with charcoal will give your drawing a dramatic, dark look, whereas shading in pencil can produce a subtler, softer appearance. And shading in ink adds a slick, smooth feel!

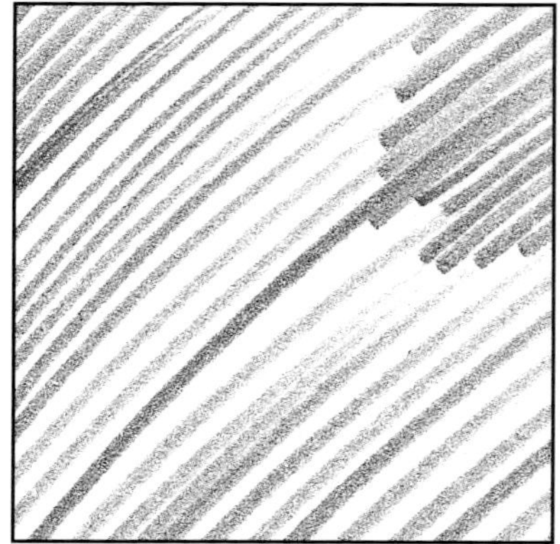

Hatching The most basic method of shading is to fill an area with hatching, which is a series of parallel strokes.

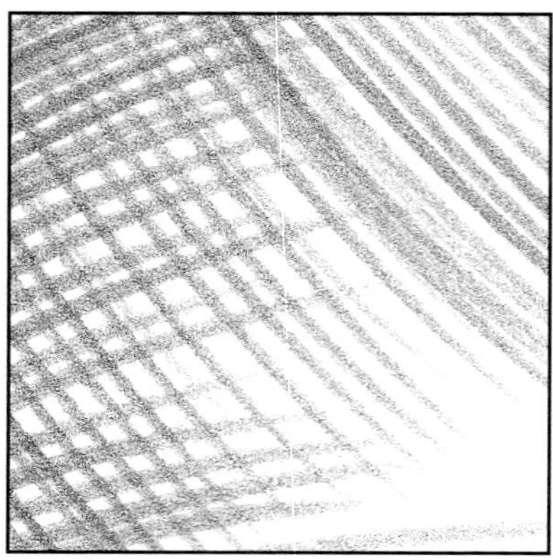

Crosshatching For darker shading, go over your hatching with a perpendicular set of hatch marks.

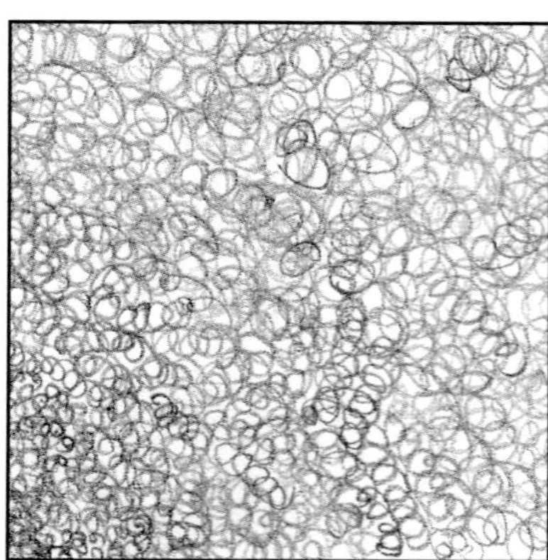

Circular Strokes By moving your pencil in tight, small circles, you can create a texture that is ideal for a mop of unruly hair.

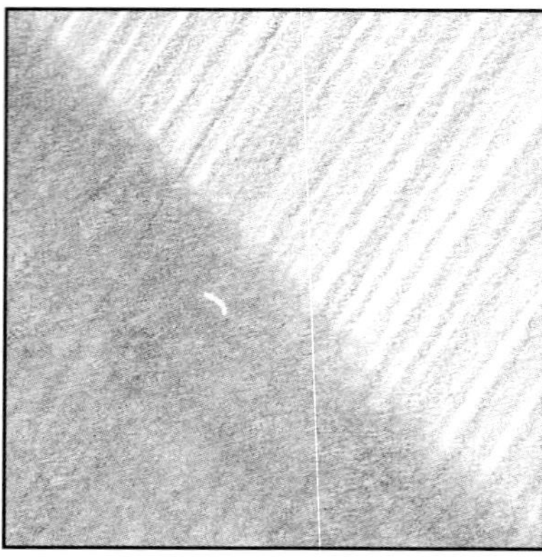

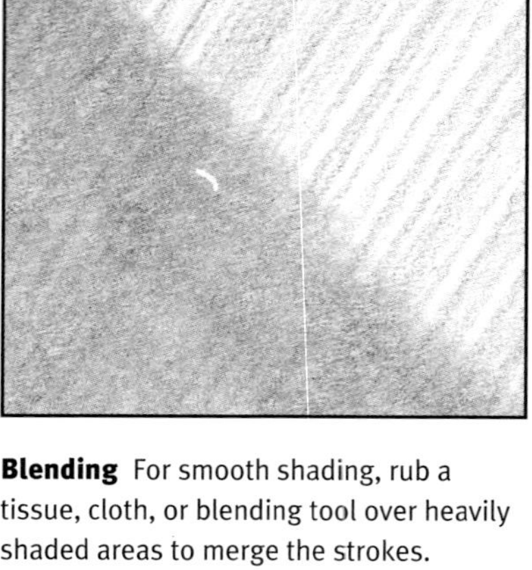

Blending For smooth shading, rub a tissue, cloth, or blending tool over heavily shaded areas to merge the strokes.

Stippling A series of dots can create a mottled texture for skin, scales, and hair; the denser the dots, the darker the tone.

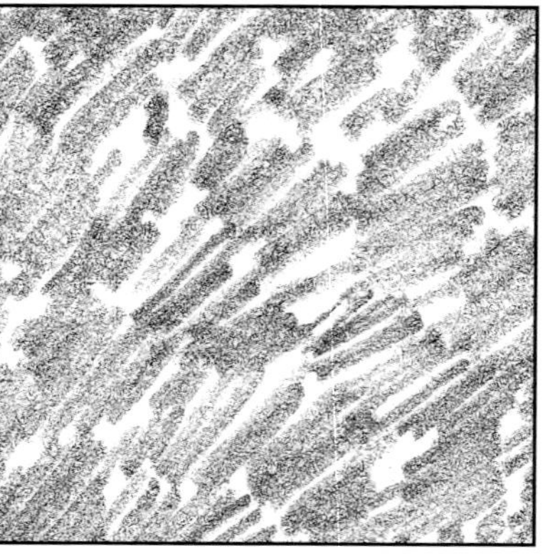

Scribbling To create loose, spontaneous strokes, hastily move the pencil around in quick, random motions.

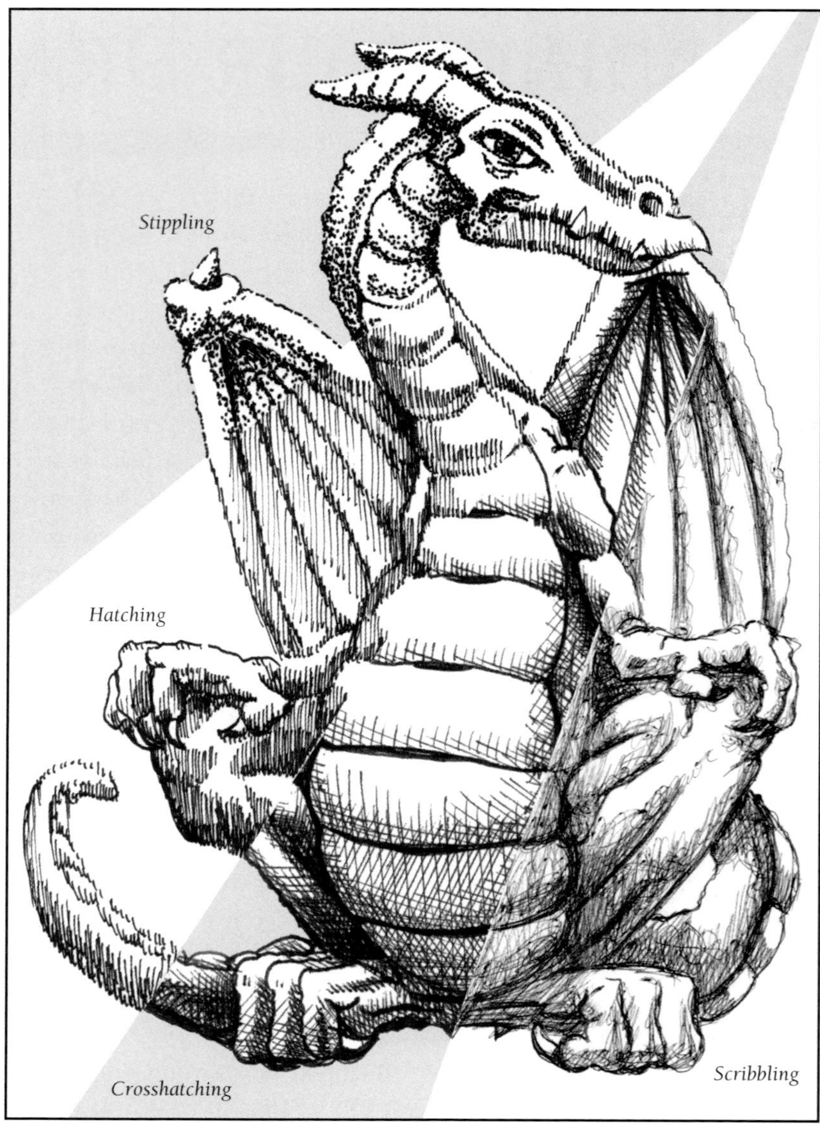

Putting Ink Strokes to Use In this sectioned drawing, you can see how each shading technique results in a different look and feel for the finished piece. In the uppermost section, I stipple with an ultra-fine permanent marker to create dynamic shadows; for darker values, I apply denser dots. For the next area, I use a .3 mm ink pen to create closely spaced hatch marks that suggest a rough texture. I crosshatch the next section with a .5 mm ink pen to create a rough, scaly look. For the final section, I build up a loose scribble with a ballpoint pen to achieve a cracked, worn texture.

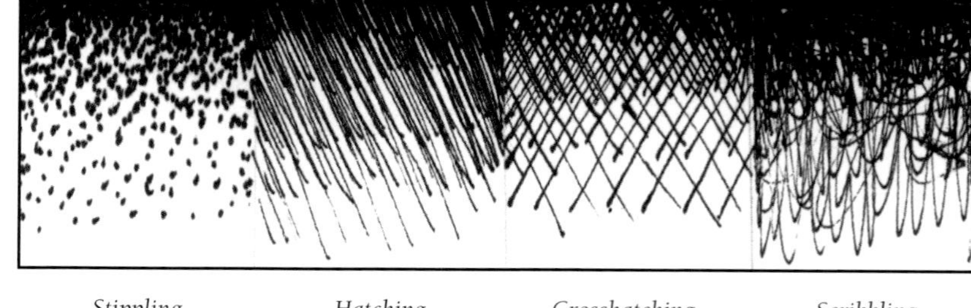

Using Ink You can use the same shading techniques with ink as those used with pencil, as the example above demonstrates. However, ink is a much less forgiving medium than pencil—you cannot erase your marks. To avoid making mistakes, sketch the entire drawing (including details) in pencil first; then apply the ink. When the ink is completely dry, gently go over the entire drawing with an eraser to pick up any stray pencil marks. If you've diluted the ink to a wash, be sure to allow more time for drying.

Varying Values with Paint and Ink Washes

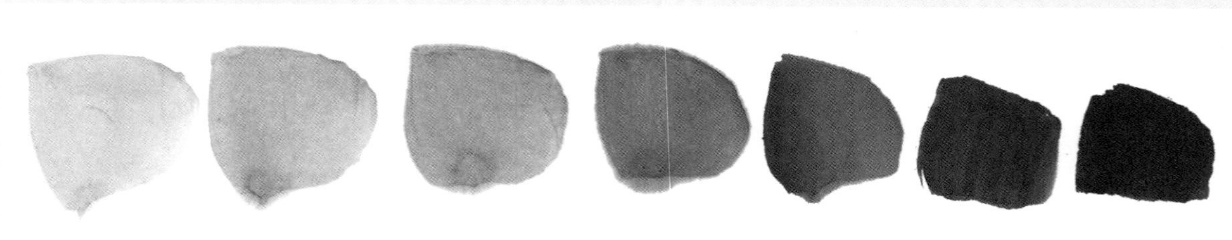

Adjusting the amount of water you use in your ink or paint washes provides a range of values. When creating a wash, it is best to start with the lightest value and build up to a darker value, rather than adding water to a dark wash to lighten it. To learn how to mix various values, create a value chart like this one. Start with a very diluted wash, and gradually add more ink or paint for successively darker values.

Creating Textures

Practicing the techniques shown below will help you create the appearance of textures such as scales and feathers—features you'll find on the dragons throughout this book. It's often helpful to use a photo reference of a real human or animal with features similar to those you want to depict for your creatures. For example, look at patterns on turtle shells and fish for scale inspiration!

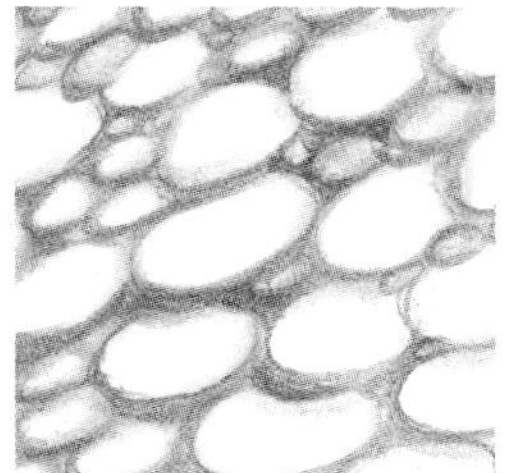

Smooth Scales For smooth scales, first draw irregularly shaped ovals; then shade between them. Smooth scales like these are ideal for the slick skin of sea-dwelling dragons.

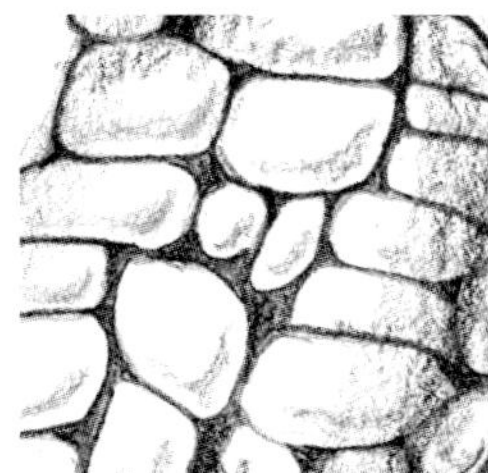

Rough Scales To create rough scales, draw irregular shapes that follow a slightly curved alignment. Shade darkly between the shapes; then shade over them with light, parallel strokes.

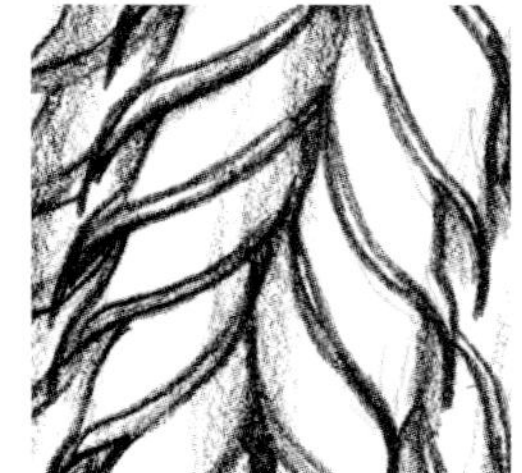

Spiny Scales For sharp, pointed scales, sketch the form with a 2H pencil, adding details with a black colored pencil. Lightly grip the pencil to create softly curving arcs for the differently shaped spines.

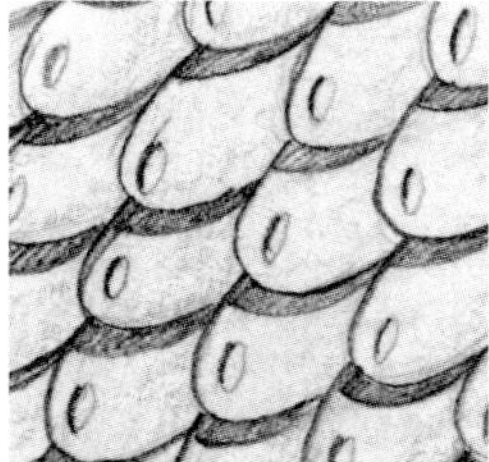

Fishlike Scales To depict scales such as those found on most Asian dragons, draw arcs of various sizes. Partially cover each scale with the next layer, and add a cast shadow below each to show overlap.

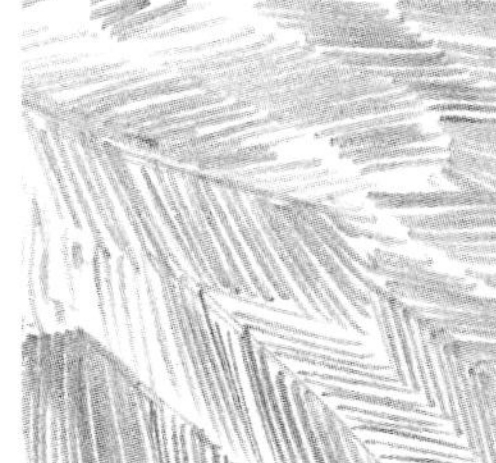

Fine Feathers For light, downy feathers, apply thin, parallel lines along the feather stems, forming a series of V shapes. Avoid crisp outlines, which would take away from the softness.

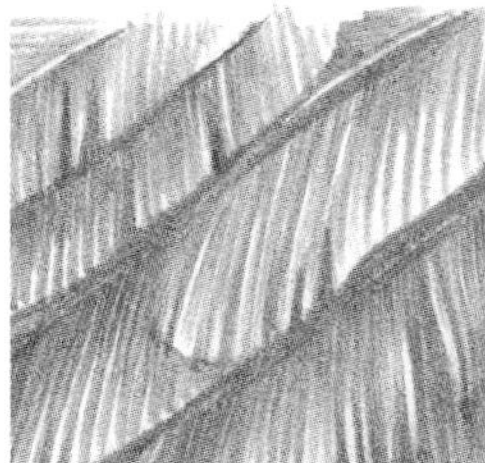

Heavy Feathers To create thicker, more defined feathers, use heavier parallel strokes and blend with a tortillon. Apply the most graphite to the shadowed areas between the feathers.

Constructing Creatures

Approaching a drawing becomes a much simpler process when you begin by breaking down the subject into basic *forms*, or three-dimensional shapes. And these simple shapes, with a little refinement, easily can become body parts of your creature. In my drawings, cylinders often act as the underlying forms of legs, and cubes usually become feet. (See the examples below for a demonstration of this drawing method.) That's all there is to the first step of every drawing: sketching the shapes and developing the forms. After that, it's just a matter of connecting and refining the lines and adding details.

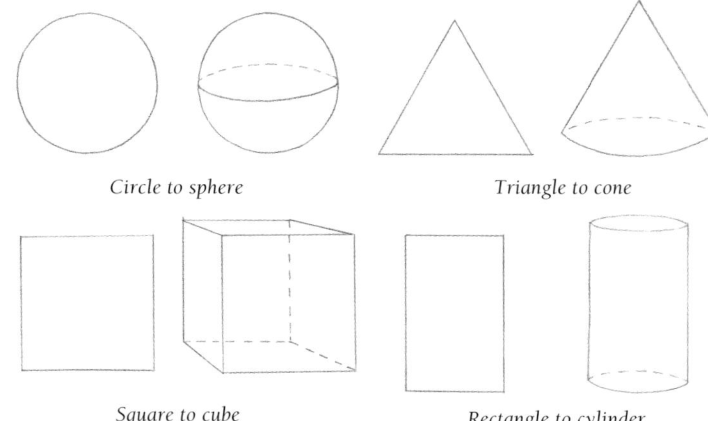

Transforming Shapes into Forms Here I've drawn the four basic shapes and their respective forms. I think of the shapes as flat frontal views of the forms; when tipped, they appear as three-dimensional forms. Use ellipses to show the backs of the circle, cylinder, and cone; draw a cube by connecting two squares with parallel lines.

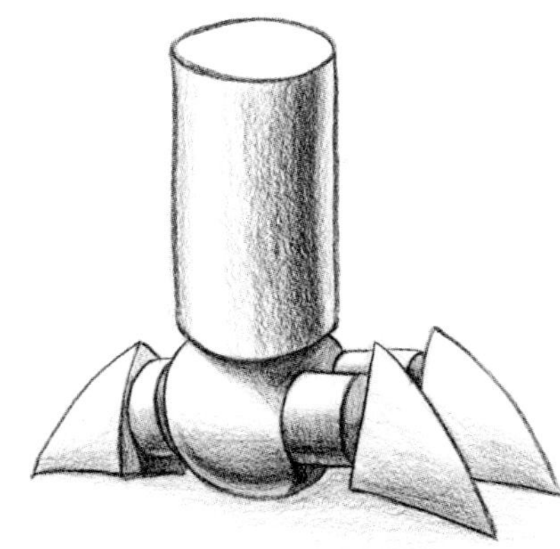

Starting with Shapes This is what a dragon foot would look like rendered entirely with geometric forms. I use cylinders for the leg, a circle for the ball of the foot, and triangle shapes for the claws.

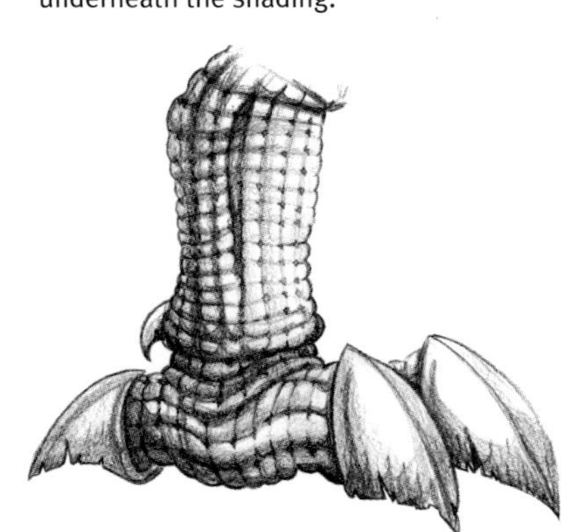

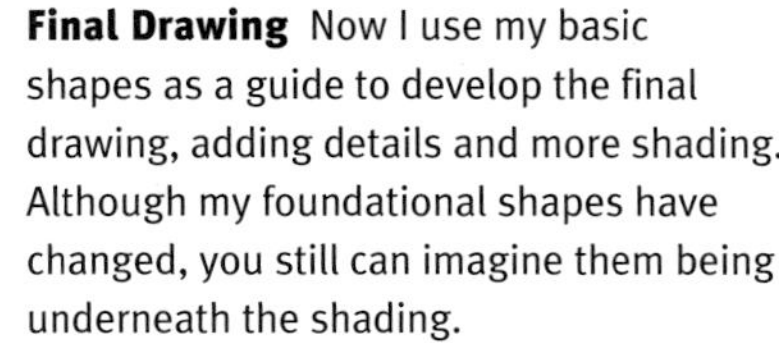

Final Drawing Now I use my basic shapes as a guide to develop the final drawing, adding details and more shading. Although my foundational shapes have changed, you still can imagine them being underneath the shading.

Transforming Basic Shapes

Here is an example of the way I use simple shapes and forms to develop a dragon. In the first step, I use a circle for the head, an oval for the torso, and cylinders for the legs. In the next step, I connect the shapes and erase the guidelines to develop the forms of the body. I also add facial features and define the snout. In the third step, I build up the shapes and forms to refine the body, adding details such as the plates and toenails and erasing my construction lines as I draw.

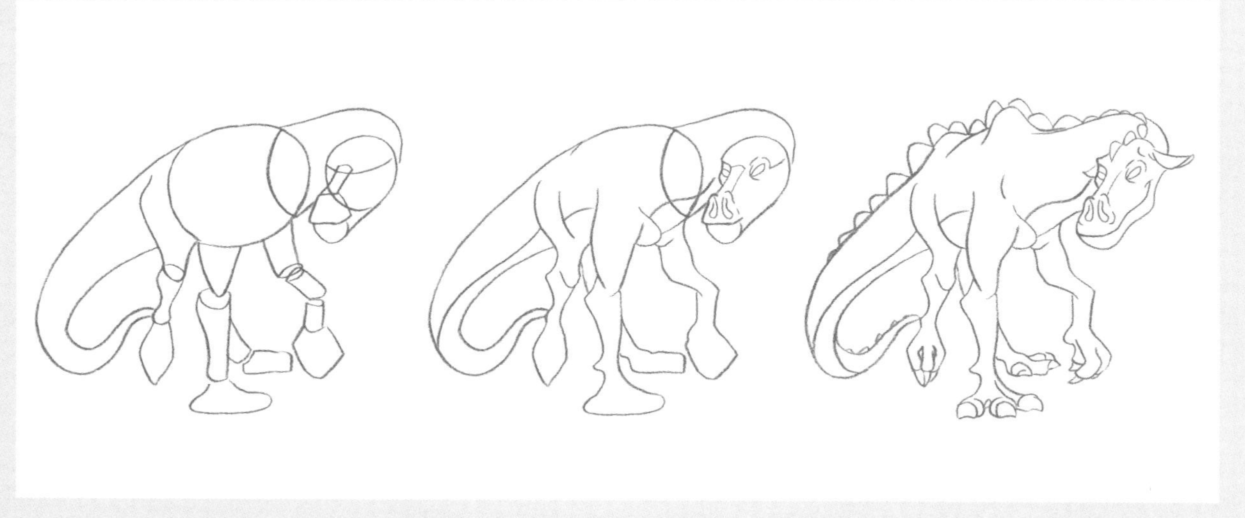

Fire Dragon

Elemental dragons are those that are related to the elemental spheres: fire, earth, air, and water. These dragons tend to personify their respective element. The fire dragon is the most unpredictable of the elementals. Often dwelling in dormant volcanoes, this dragon is red, orange, or yellow in color. Its body is thick and heavy, and its legs and tail are long and snakelike.

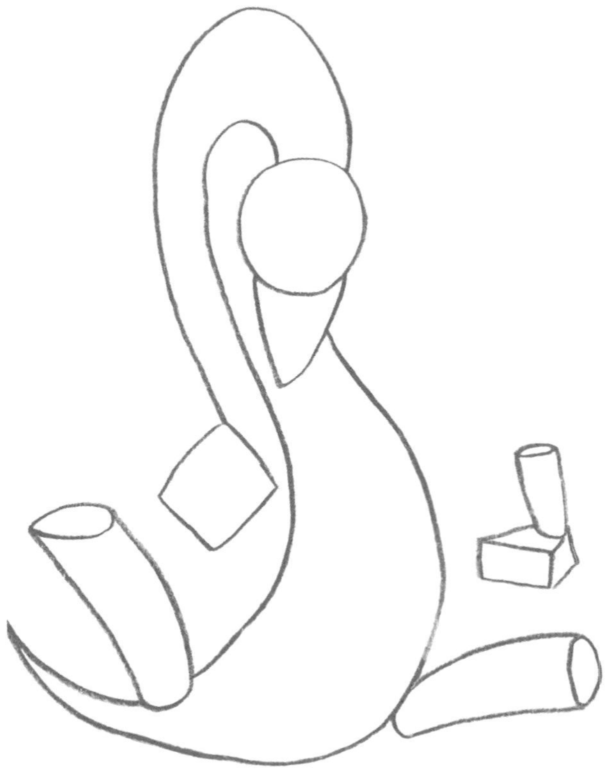

Step One I begin drawing the fire dragon using a 2H pencil and basic shapes. I start with an S shape for the body, adding a circle and a triangle for the head. Then I draw cylindrical legs and boxlike hands.

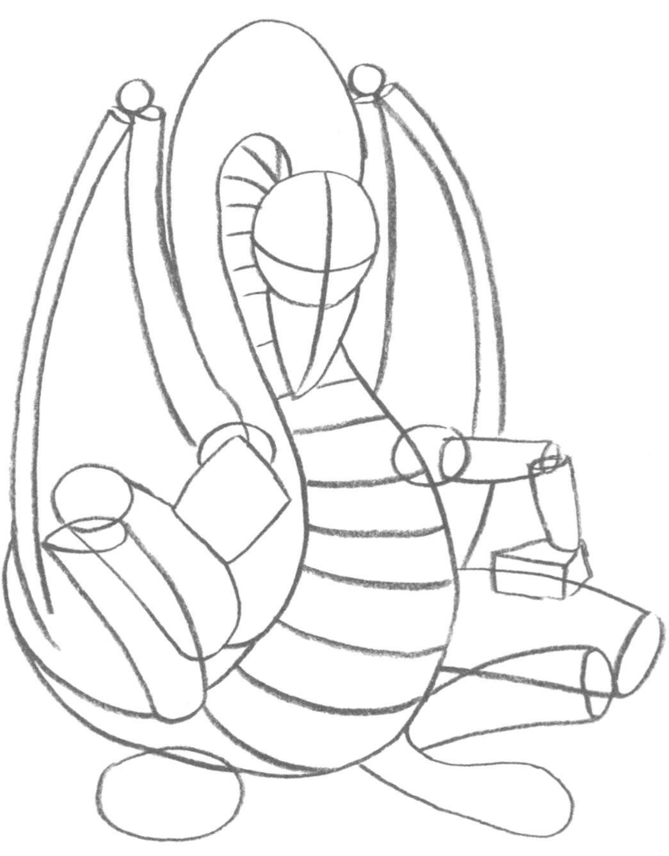

Step Two I add more cylindrical shapes to form the legs and arms. I rough in the feet and the wings, using long, tapered lines and circles. I add horizontal lines down the belly. Then I add horizontal and vertical facial guidelines to help me place the features.

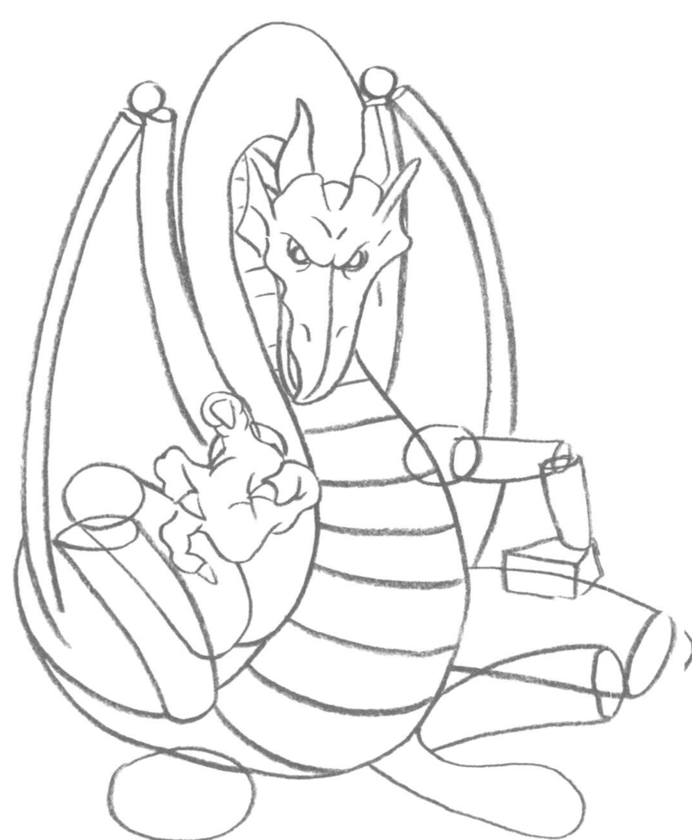

Step Three Now I focus on the head. I add two curved horns and the wide ears, and I draw the sloping eyes and the birdlike beak, erasing guidelines as they're no longer needed. Next I develop the reaching hand, converting the box shape from step one into the palm. I draw pointed fingers, complete with long nails. Notice that the hand is almost as big as the head—this is an example of *foreshortening,* in which the drawing is distorted to make certain areas of the drawing (in this case, the hand) appear to be closer to the viewer than other parts. Foreshortening helps create the appearance of depth.

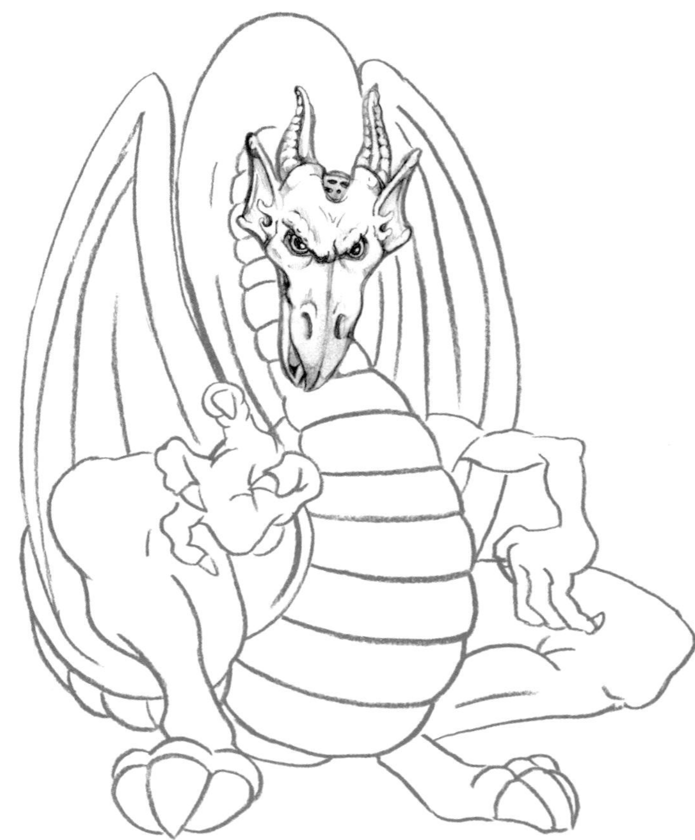

Step Four Using my construction lines as a guide, I draw the muscular legs, the thin arm, the fingers on the dragon's left hand, and the large, pointed toes. I also add a curve to each segment of the belly to make it look three-dimensional. I refine the wings. Then, with a blunt HB pencil, I define the creases and recesses of the face. I use a sharp 2B to add tone to the ears, horns, eyes, nose, and mouth; then I add dark spots on the head.

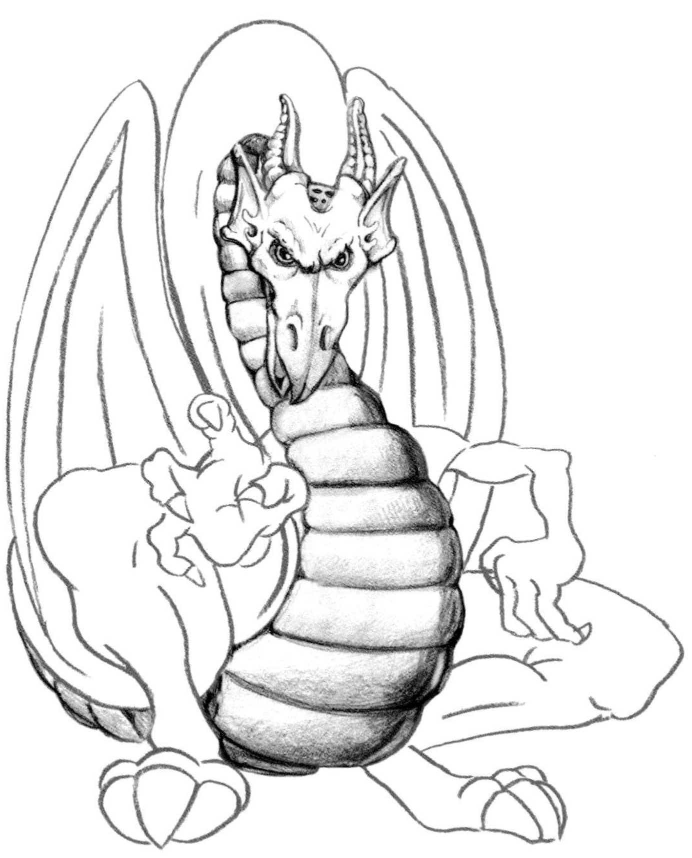

Step Five I move to the neck and belly, using a 2B pencil to shade with fine, horizontal strokes. To show that the light is coming from the left, I leave highlights along the dragon's right side, gradually darkening the value toward its left side and underbelly.

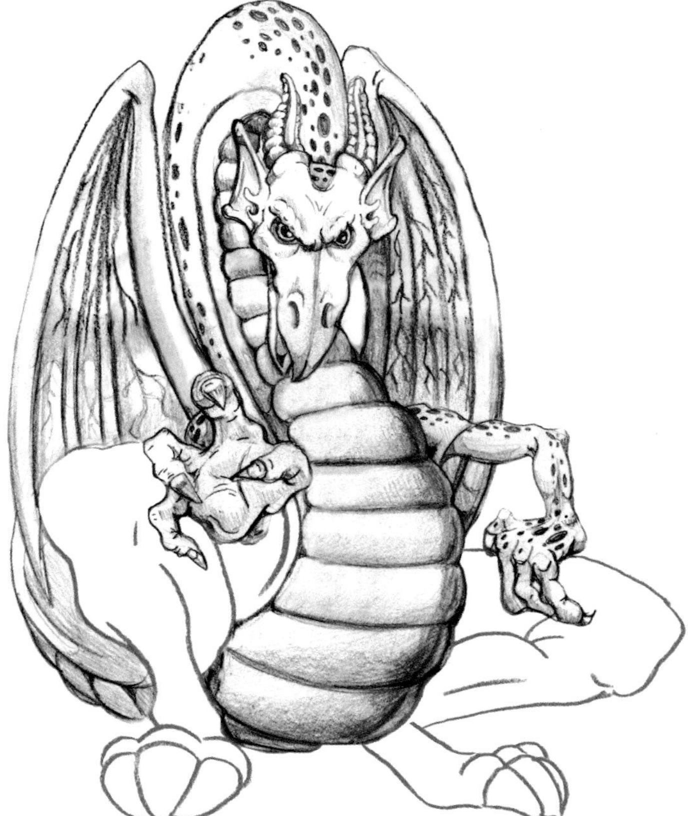

Step Six Next I shade the wings, the back of the neck, the arms, and the hands. I draw spots on the neck and arms, and I add thin, branching lines for the veins on the inner wings. Then I make short strokes for the wrinkles on the hands.

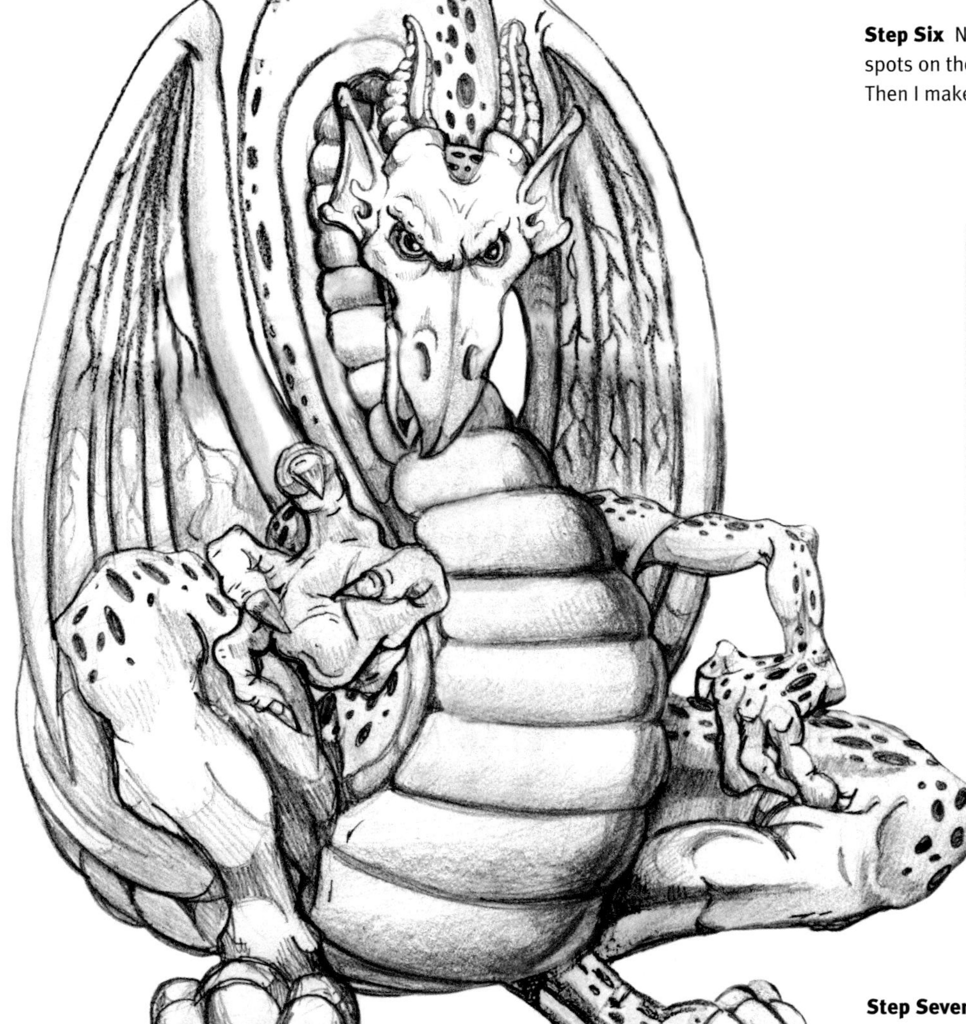

Did you know?

- In Chinese astrology, if you were born between January 31, 1976, and February 17, 1977, you were born under the sign of the Fire Dragon.
- In Greek mythology, Prometheus stole fire from the gods to protect the fireless humans, and he was tortured for his act of kindness.

Step Seven I continue shading the rest of the body with a 2B pencil. Then I add spots to the legs and the top of the dragon's left foot. I remove any remaining underlying pencil lines with an art gum eraser, and then I reinforce the darkest areas with more shading, as shown.

Water Dragon

Another elemental dragon, the water dragon usually does not have legs or wings, and thus does not fly. Blue, silver, or blue-green in color, this dragon lives in seas, lakes, rivers, and other bodies of water. The water dragon is thought to represent calm and fluidity. It has been sighted most often off the coasts of Scandinavia, the British Isles, and Denmark.

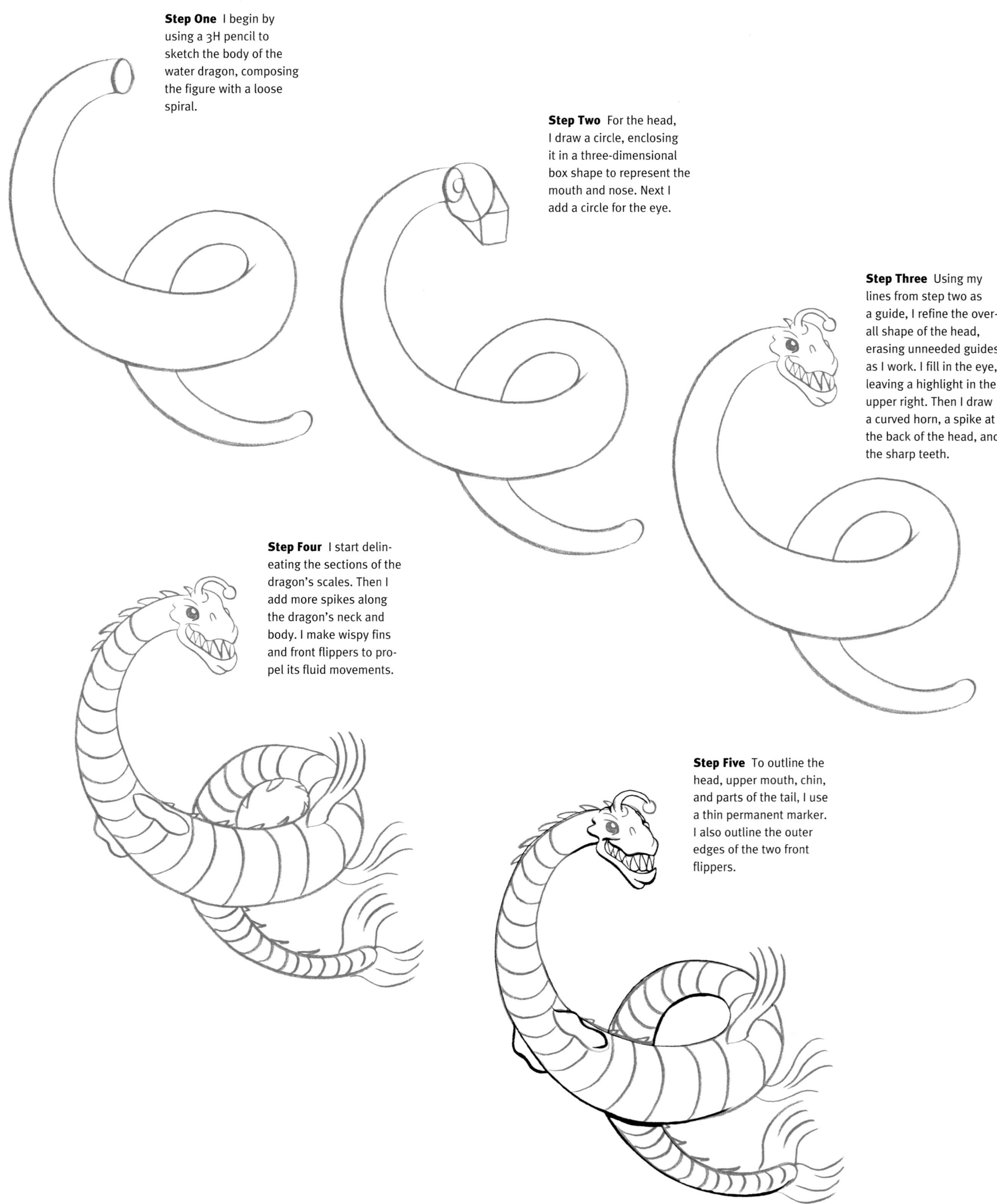

Step One I begin by using a 3H pencil to sketch the body of the water dragon, composing the figure with a loose spiral.

Step Two For the head, I draw a circle, enclosing it in a three-dimensional box shape to represent the mouth and nose. Next I add a circle for the eye.

Step Three Using my lines from step two as a guide, I refine the overall shape of the head, erasing unneeded guides as I work. I fill in the eye, leaving a highlight in the upper right. Then I draw a curved horn, a spike at the back of the head, and the sharp teeth.

Step Four I start delineating the sections of the dragon's scales. Then I add more spikes along the dragon's neck and body. I make wispy fins and front flippers to propel its fluid movements.

Step Five To outline the head, upper mouth, chin, and parts of the tail, I use a thin permanent marker. I also outline the outer edges of the two front flippers.

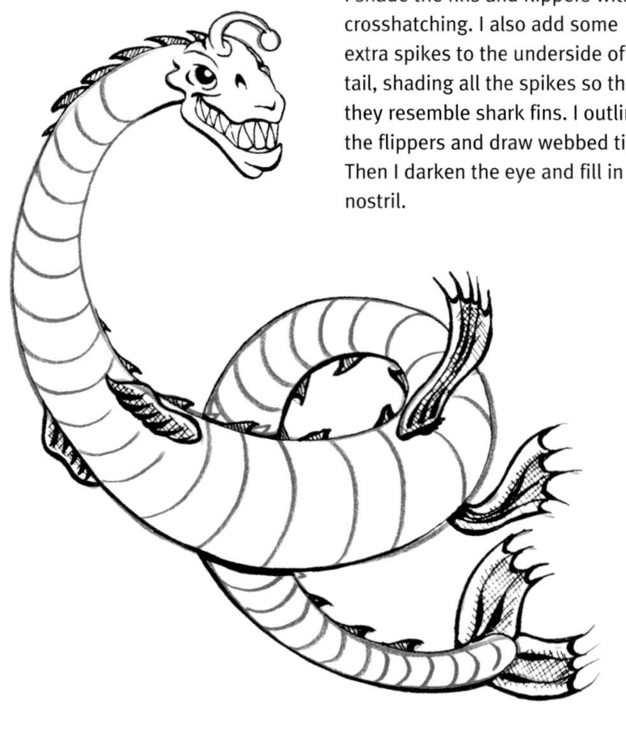

Step Six Using the same marker, I shade the fins and flippers with crosshatching. I also add some extra spikes to the underside of the tail, shading all the spikes so that they resemble shark fins. I outline the flippers and draw webbed tips. Then I darken the eye and fill in the nostril.

Step Seven I add scales and shading to the dragon's body. I think about shellfish as I draw. I put round tips on the ends of the fins and tail, perhaps as tantalizing bait for unsuspecting fish passing by.

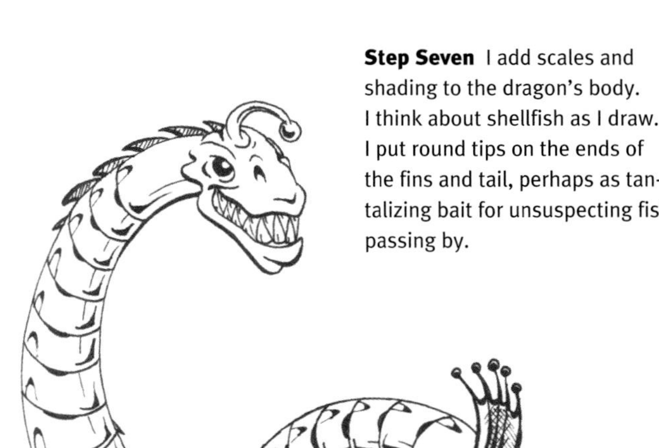

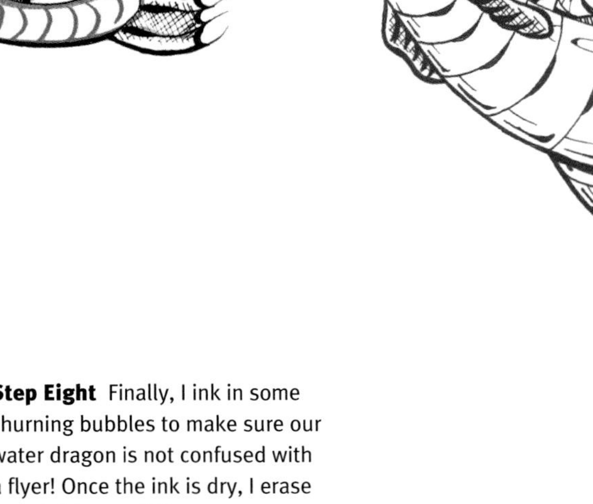

Step Eight Finally, I ink in some churning bubbles to make sure our water dragon is not confused with a flyer! Once the ink is dry, I erase any visible pencil lines.

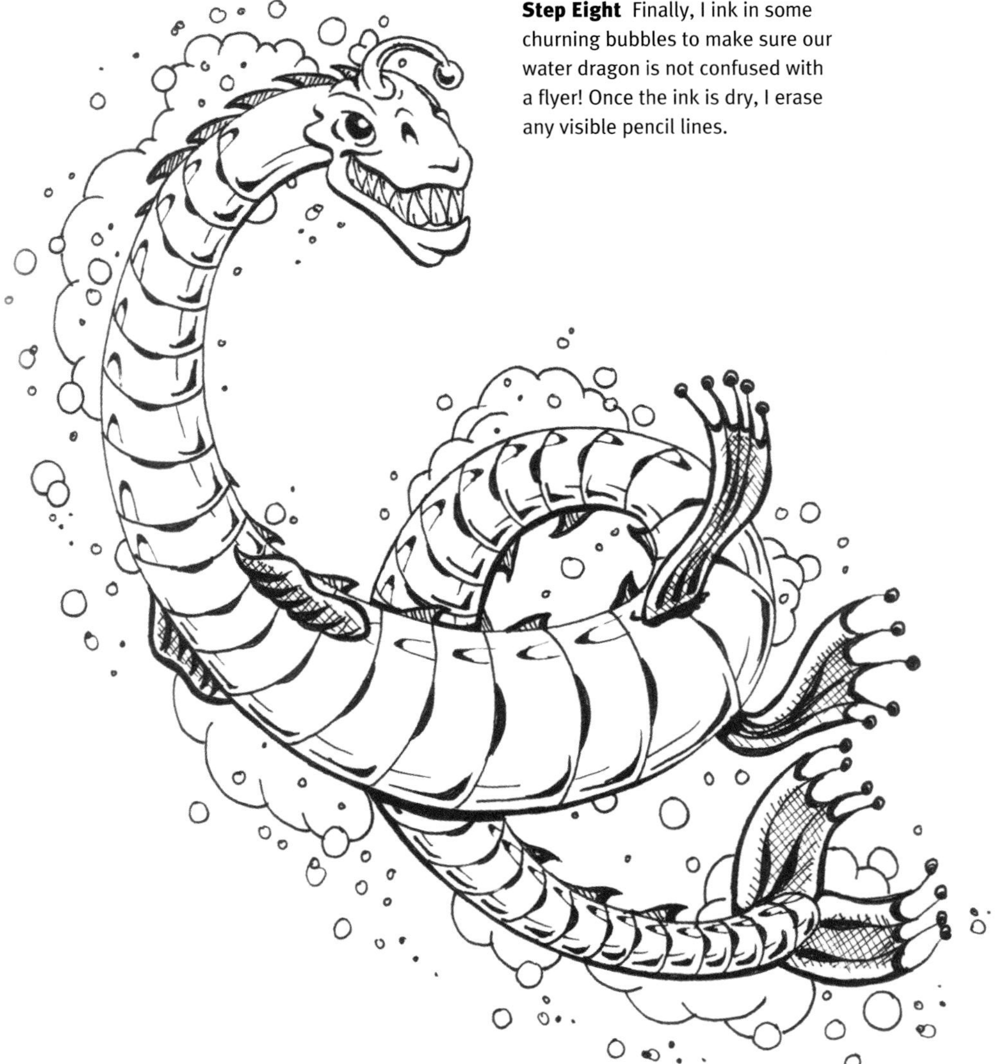

Did you know?

- There are two species of reptiles that go by the name "water dragon": One is Chinese and the other Australian. These real-life lizards are able to remain submerged for long periods of time.
- Like many lizards, the water dragon has a third eye at the top of its head.
- If you were born between January 27, 1952, and February 13, 1953, you were born under the Chinese astrological sign of the Water Dragon.

Earth Dragon

The earth dragon is the most practical and levelheaded of the elemental dragons. Usually green or brown in color, it resides in mountains and forests. The earth dragon tends to have a heavier body, with four legs, wings, and a long neck and tail. The earth dragon is very responsible and takes its life and relationships quite seriously.

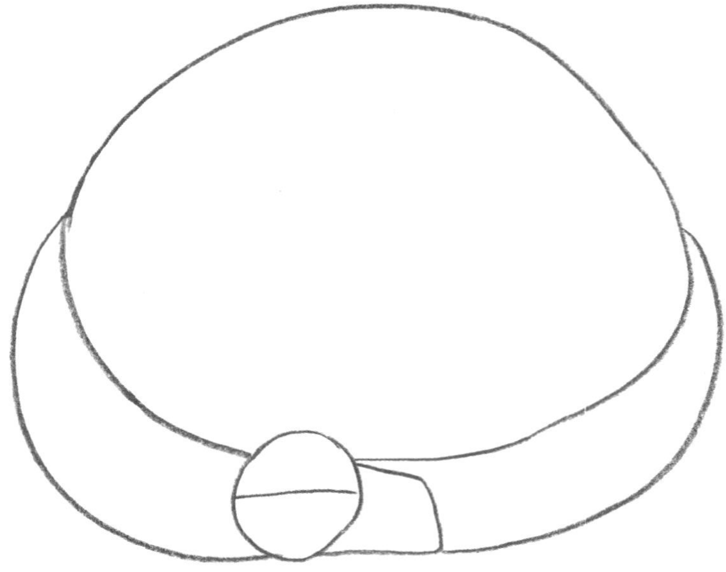

Step One I start this dragon by using a 3H pencil to make a large oval for the body. I draw a small circle at the bottom of the oval for the head, and I add a squarish shape to block in the muzzle. Then I draw two thicker, curved lines outside the oval for the neck and tail. I draw a horizontal guideline through the head for feature placement.

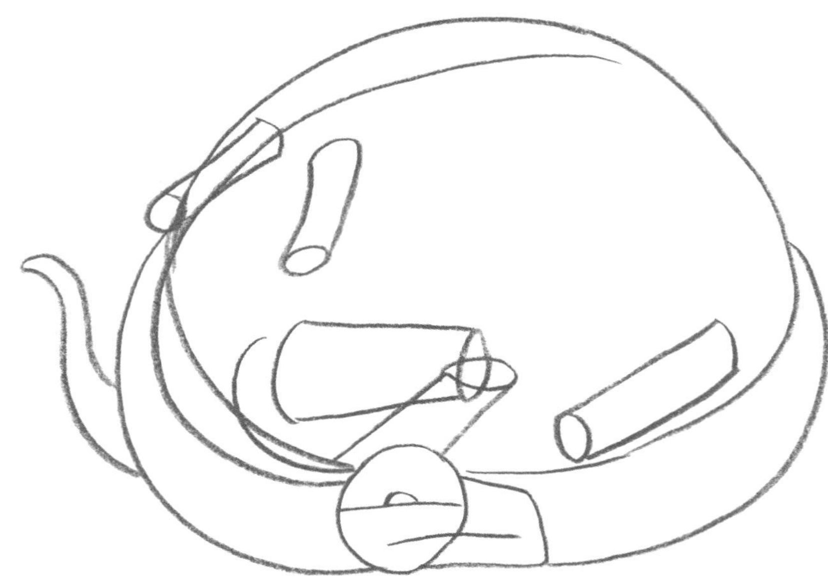

Step Two I block in the forms of the wings and legs with cylindrical shapes. I also draw a half-circle at the horizontal guideline for the eye, and I add another line that bisects the nose to suggest the mouth. Then I add the tip of the tail.

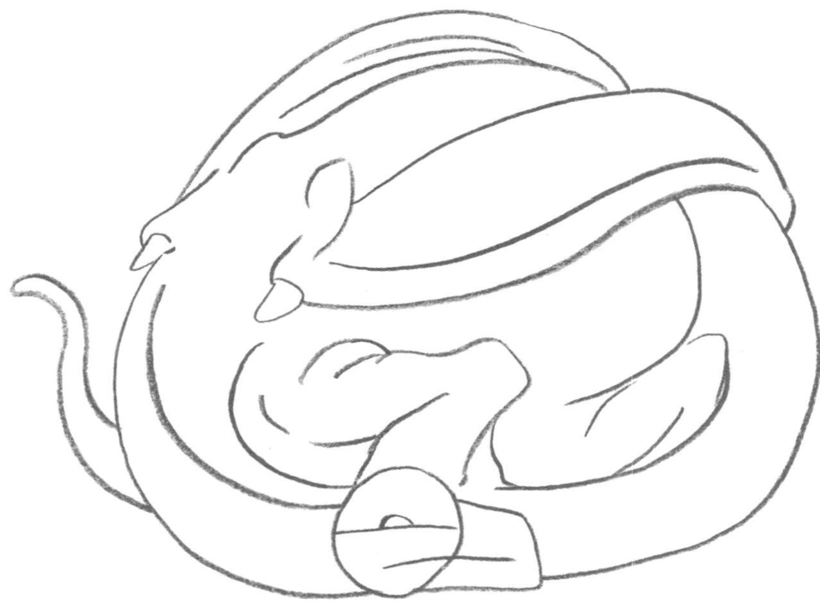

Step Three Using my construction lines, I refine the shapes to make the basic outline of the dragon, adding two wings folding over the body. I add horns to the tops of the wings, and I erase any guidelines I no longer need. Follow the example to refine your own drawing.

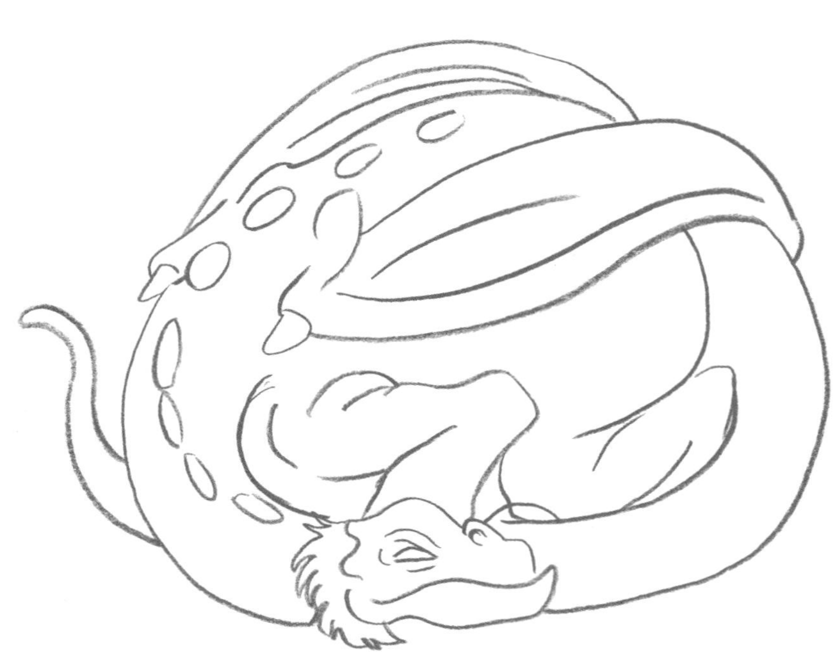

Step Four Moving to the head, I draw a curved line for the lower jaw, creating an underbite. Then I add the spiky hair, nose, and eye details. I also draw a series of oval shapes for the spikes down the dragon's neck and over its back.

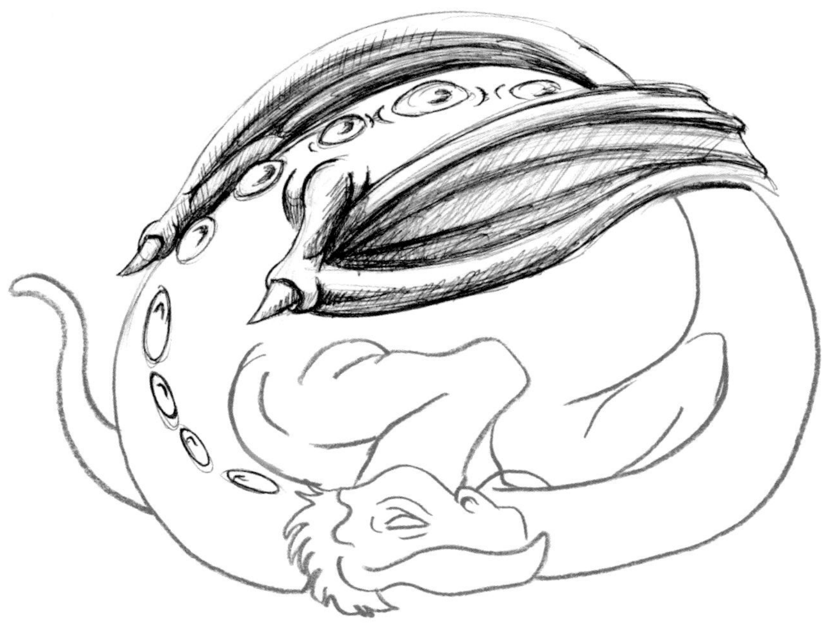

Step Five I want to achieve a very dark value for this dragon, so I decide to use a black ballpoint pen to add tone. I start with the wings, using a scribbling motion. The idea behind this technique is similar to hatching: The tighter the lines, the darker the tone. However, these lines are put down in a faster, more haphazard fashion. This is scribbling at its finest!

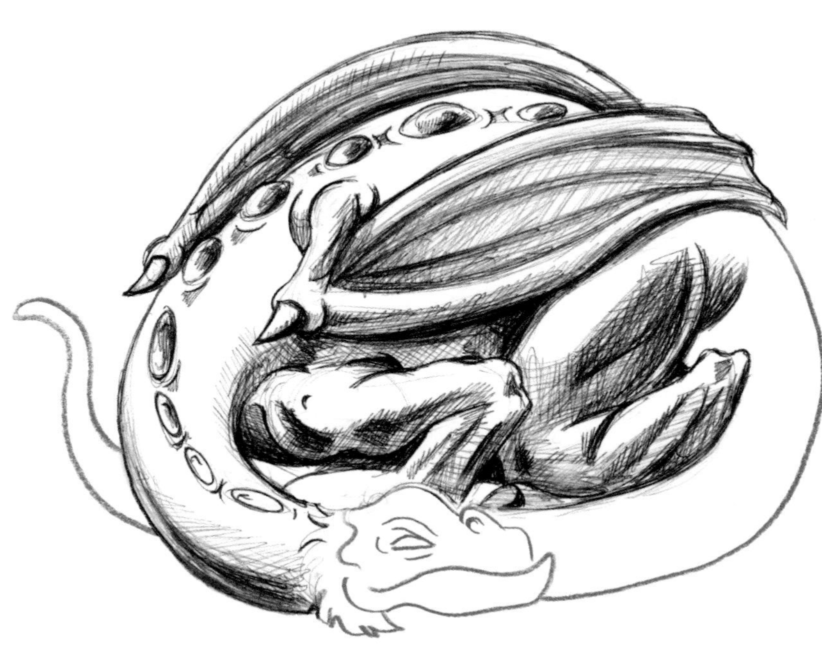

Step Six I continue the scribble-hatch on the limbs, and I apply tone to the spikes on the back, working my way toward the head. I add some hatching to the underside of the neck, as well.

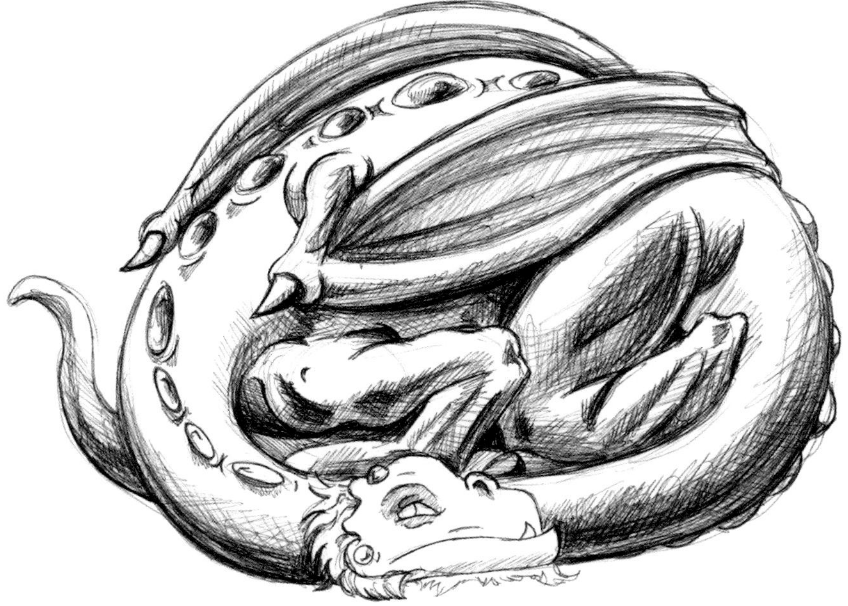

Step Seven I continue the scribble-hatch to shade the rest of the dragon's body, including the end of the tail. I also add bumps to the backside of the tail. As I approach the head, I need to think about what personality I want the dragon to have. This is going to be a tired dragon, old and world-weary. I extend his hair tuft to reach under his chin and begin to express deep, somber eyes.

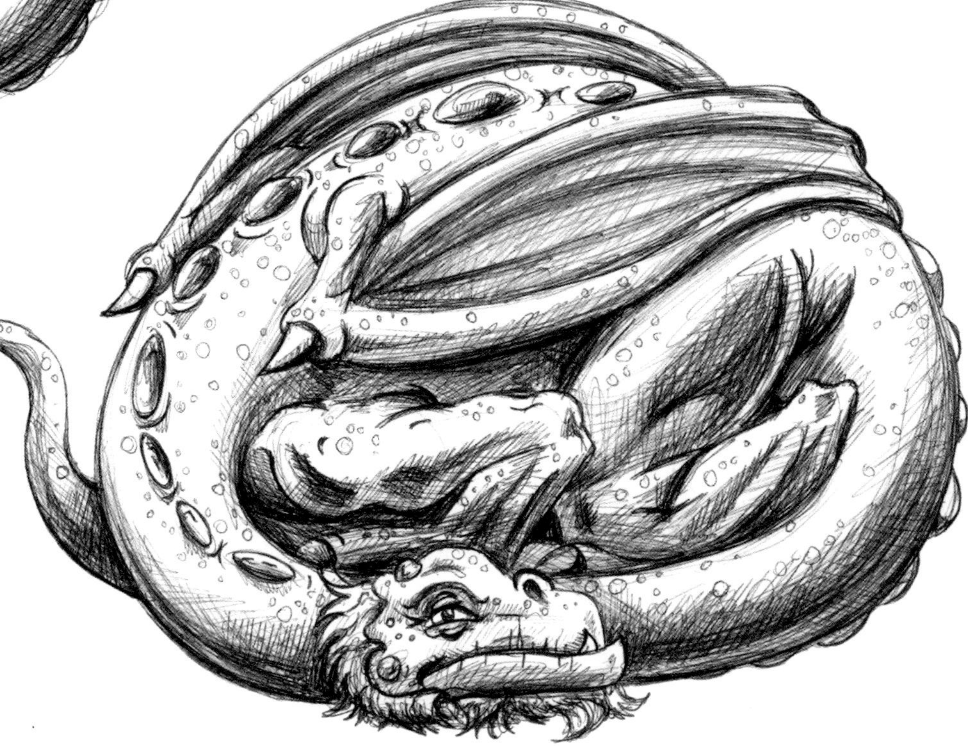

Step Eight To finish, I add simple circles to the dragon's skin, giving it a rougher texture. I also reinforce the tangled mess of fur on the head. Then I continue refining the facial features, adding creases and cracks to produce a worn appearance.

Did you know?

- If you were born between February 6, 1988, and February 5, 1989, you were born under the Chinese astrological sign of the Earth Dragon.
- In magic, Earth represents strength, abundance, and stability—characteristics of the earth dragon.

Hatchling

A hatchling is a baby dragon—not to be confused with a dragonet, which is a miniature adult dragon. A group of dragon eggs is called a "clutch."

Step One I start by sketching the oval of the hatchling's egg. Although I know most of this shape will change, it helps me achieve the right proportions by drawing the entire shape. I use a 2H pencil to create the form of the hatchling with basic shapes. This sketch acts as a "blueprint" to ensure a plausible interaction between the hatchling and its environment.

Step Two Once I'm happy with my "blueprint," I erase my construction marks. Then I refine the body. I make the pointed snout reminiscent of an alligator, and I draw the curled tongue and sharp teeth. I give my creature a birdlike chest and long, thin arms with taloned hands. Next I add the areas of sticky fluid that give the hatchling that "just born" look.

Step Three Switching to a 2B, I shade and refine the hatchling. I add details on the face first, accentuating the ridges around the mouth and eye. Then I shade the iris and the large pupil. I create texture on the body, using horizontal lines near the neck and curved lines through the chest and belly. Next I shade the tail and the pointed talons, and I add a sharp spike on the elbow.

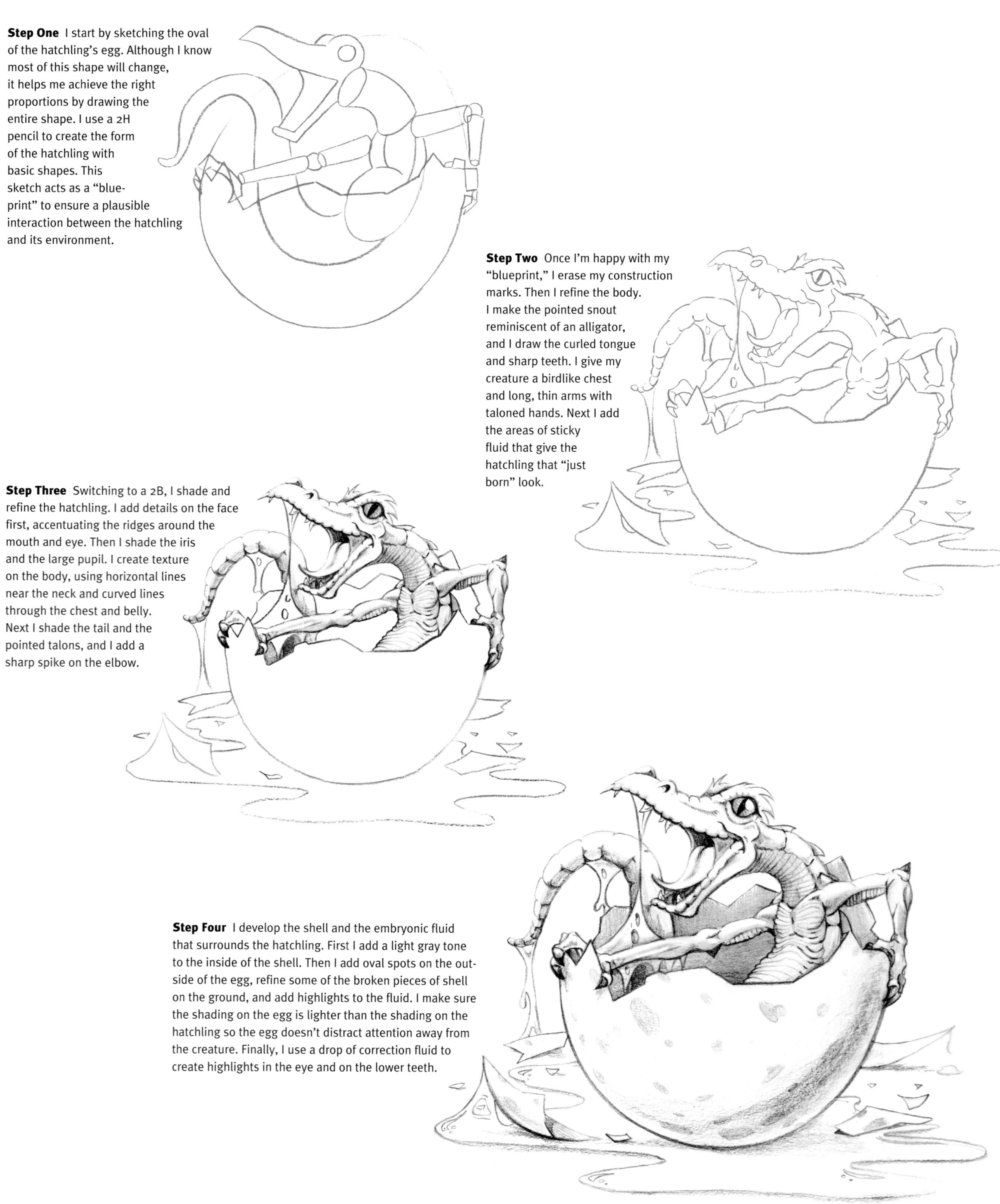

Step Four I develop the shell and the embryonic fluid that surrounds the hatchling. First I add a light gray tone to the inside of the shell. Then I add oval spots on the outside of the egg, refine some of the broken pieces of shell on the ground, and add highlights to the fluid. I make sure the shading on the egg is lighter than the shading on the hatchling so the egg doesn't distract attention away from the creature. Finally, I use a drop of correction fluid to create highlights in the eye and on the lower teeth.

Naga

Although not a true dragon, the half-human, half-serpent naga performed the same roles and functions of mythological dragons in ancient civilizations that lacked dragon lore.

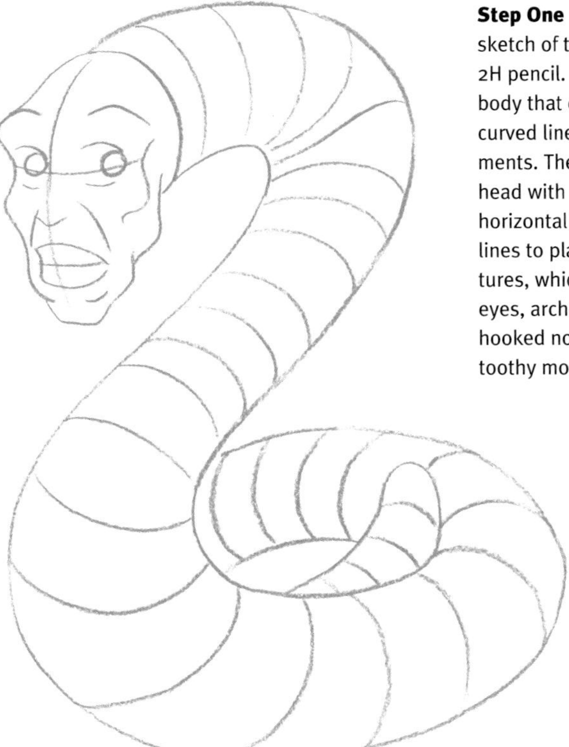

Step One I begin with a rough sketch of the creature using a 2H pencil. I draw a wormlike body that curls around, with curved lines to define the segments. Then I add a human head with a large jaw. I use horizontal and vertical guidelines to place the facial features, which include round eyes, arched eyebrows, a hooked nose, and a wide, toothy mouth.

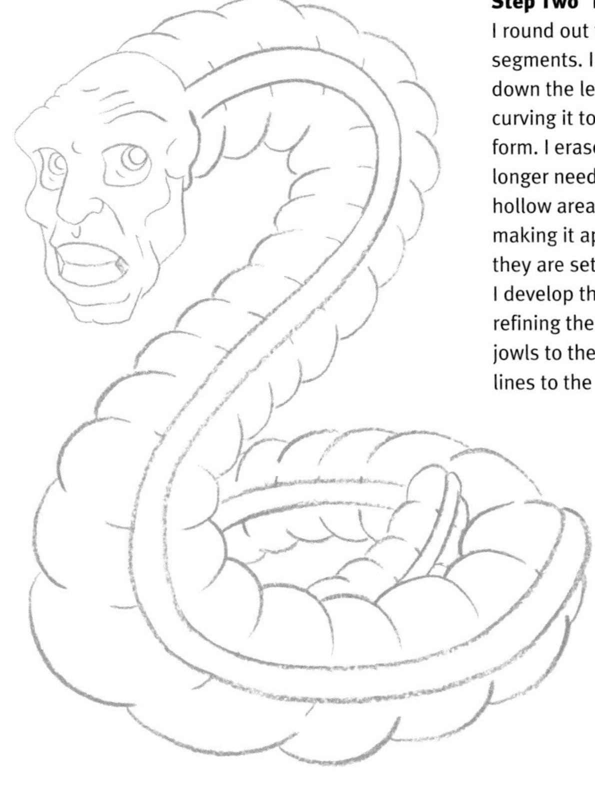

Step Two To refine the body, I round out the curves of the segments. I draw a thick ridge down the length of the body, curving it to match the body's form. I erase any lines I no longer need. Then I add a hollow area around each eye, making it appear as though they are set back into the face. I develop the nose and begin refining the mouth. I also add jowls to the cheeks and crease lines to the forehead.

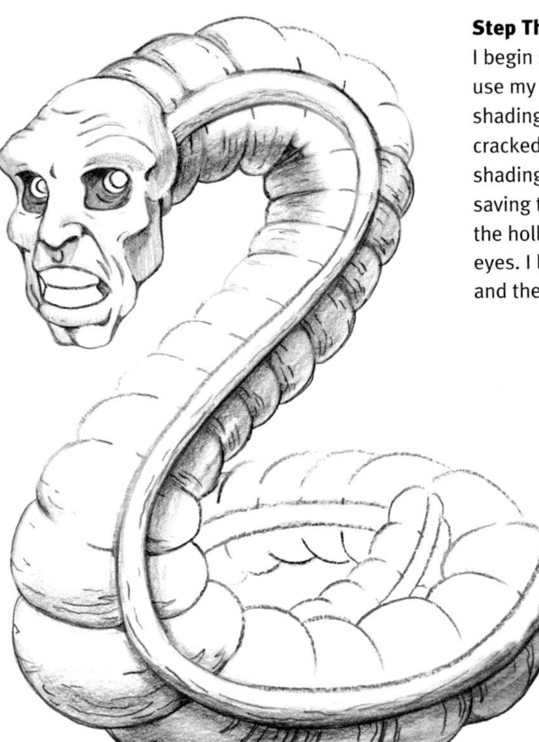

Step Three With a 2B pencil, I begin shading the body. I use my finger to smudge the shading, and then dash in cracked lines on top of the shading. Next I shade the face, saving the darkest values for the hollowed-out areas of the eyes. I leave the actual eyes and the teeth pure white.

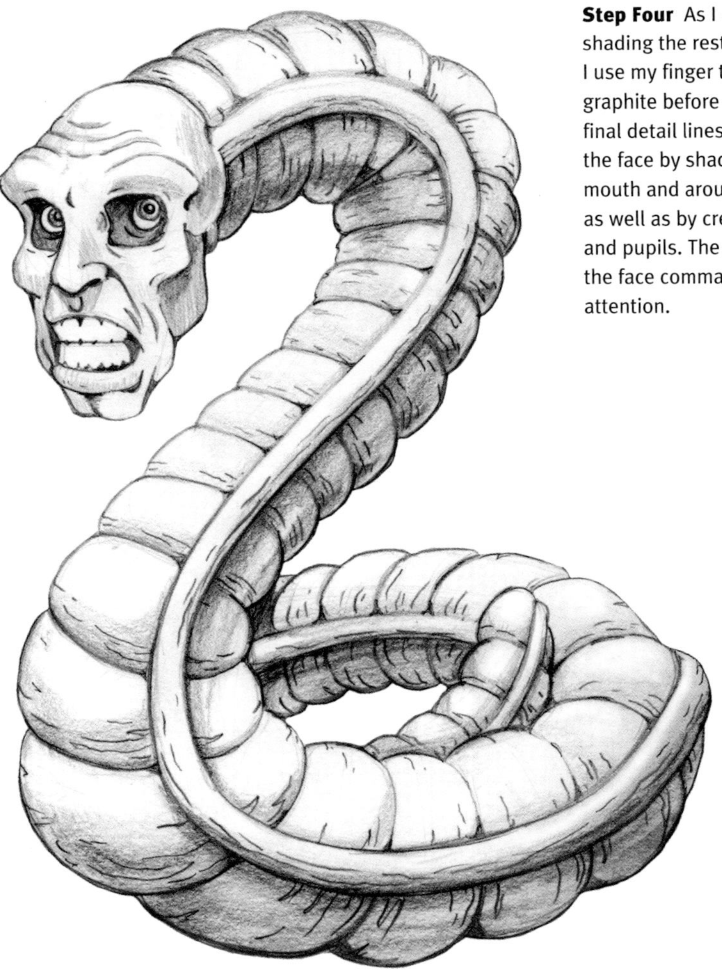

Step Four As I continue shading the rest of the body, I use my finger to smudge the graphite before adding the final detail lines. I further refine the face by shading inside the mouth and around the teeth, as well as by creating the iris and pupils. The crisp edges of the face command the viewer's attention.

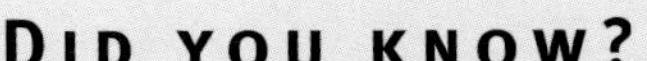

Did you know?

- In India, nagas are underground dwellers.
- The word "naga" is rooted in Sanskrit and means "serpent."
- Nagas can cause flooding or drought at will.

Drake

Often mistaken for an adolescent dragon, the drake is merely a type of dragon without wings. (Dragons' wings do not grow until adulthood.) A drake usually is referred to by its element, such as the earthdrake shown here.

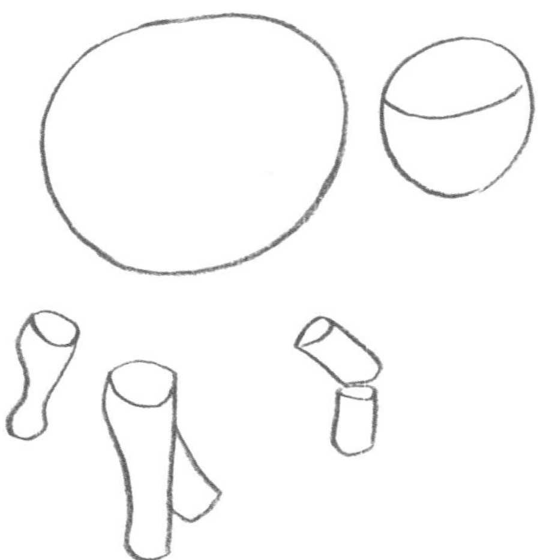

Step One I start by drawing the basic shapes of the drake with a 3H pencil. I draw an oval for the torso and a circle for the head. Then I block in the legs. Notice that I am not connecting any of these shapes yet. I add a curved horizontal guideline to the head, which indicates that the drake will be looking to the viewer's left.

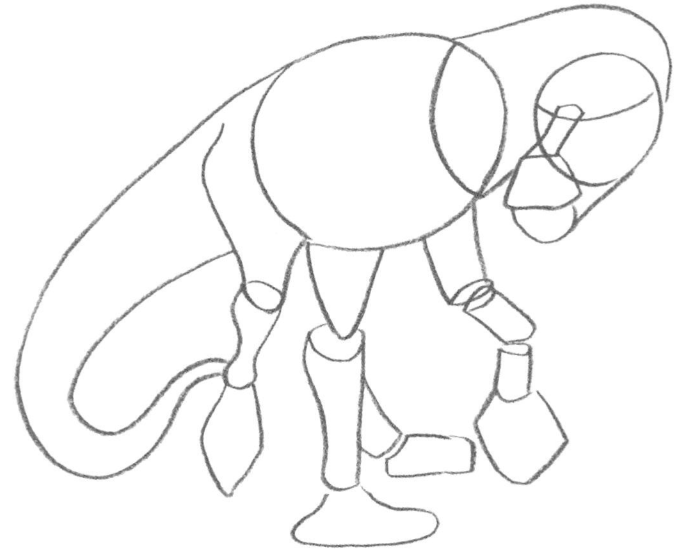

Step Two Now I add the rest of the basic shapes. I connect the shapes to form the thick snout and jaw, the curved neck, the large tail, and the bulky feet.

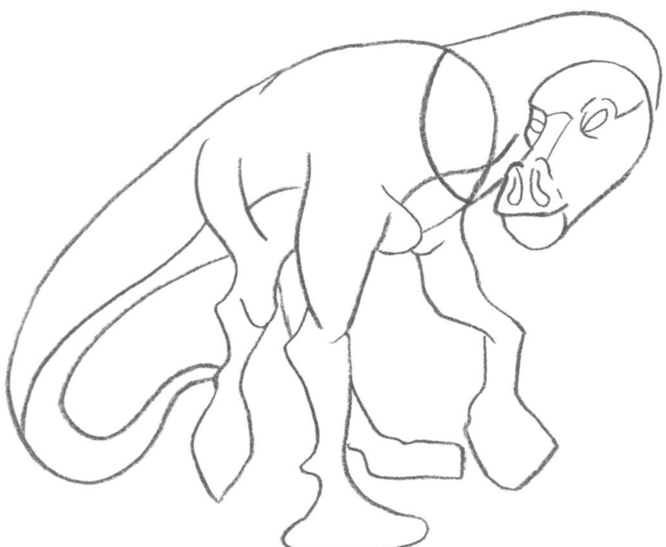

Step Three I begin to refine the body, tail, legs, and feet, erasing my construction lines as I go. Then I start rendering the facial features, including the large, cowlike nostrils.

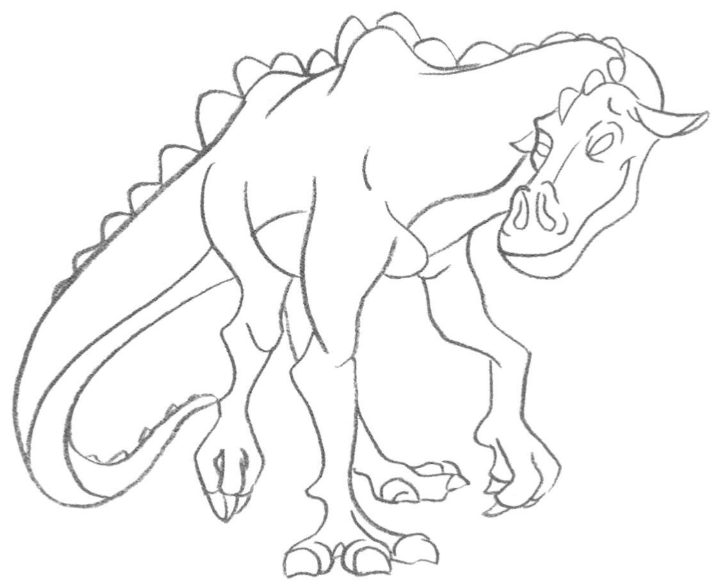

Step Four As I add the curved mouth and the floppy ears, I continue imagining a cow. Then I think of a stegosaurus as I add the plates that extend from the forehead to the tip of the tail. I refine the feet, adding three toes with long, sharp nails.

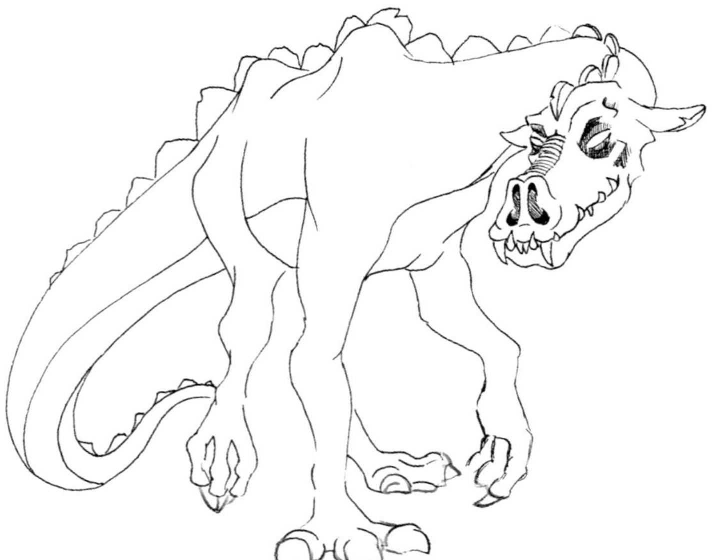

Step Five I want this drake to really stand out from the paper, so I outline my pencil sketch with .2 mm waterproof ink pen. I add details to the head, such as the pointy teeth, the ridged nose, the dark eye sockets, and the notched ear.

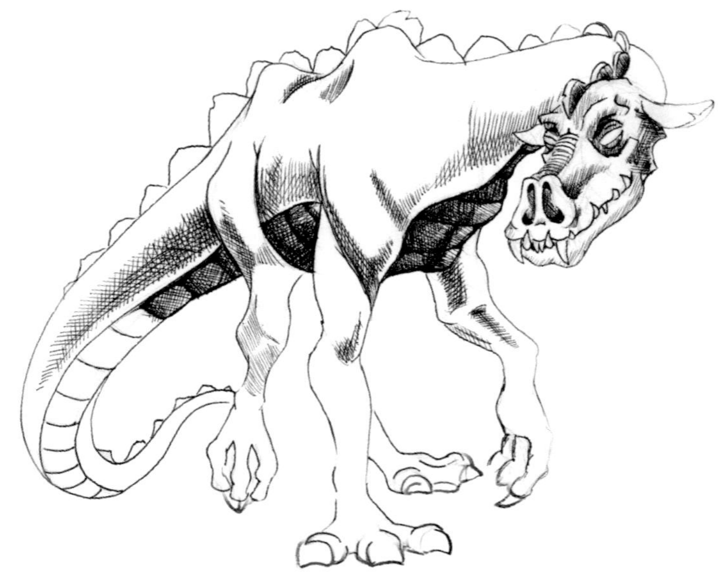

Step Six After creating horizontal lines that reach down the underside of the tail, I establish the shading on the body and head by laying down a series of hatch marks. I create darker areas, such as the underbelly, by crosshatching on top of the first layer.

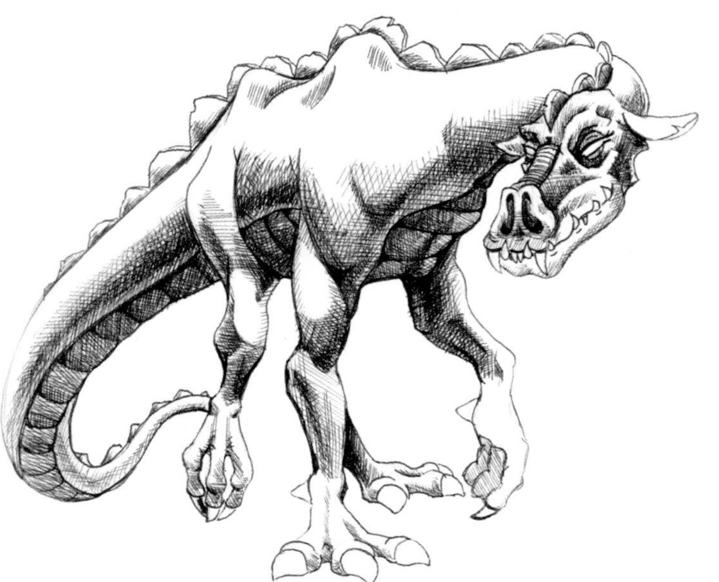

Step Seven I carry the hatch and crosshatch techniques down the limbs, onto the spine, and back to the face. Areas that may have appeared finished before may need to be revisited and strengthened so they aren't overpowered by other, less important areas.

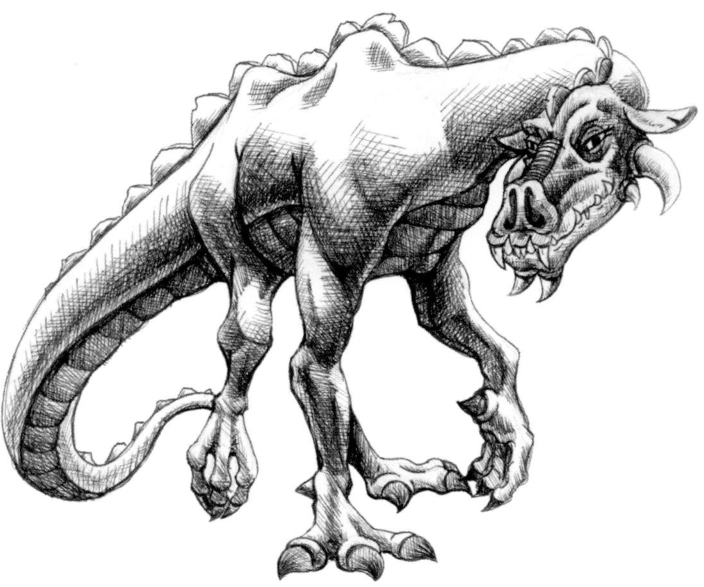

Step Eight When finished with the initial hatching on the legs and feet, I return to create darker areas. The closer the hatching, the darker the tone. Next I decide to add some details to the face, so I draw the horns on the sides of the face and the two spikes underneath the chin. I also fill in the pupil and darken the notch in the ear.

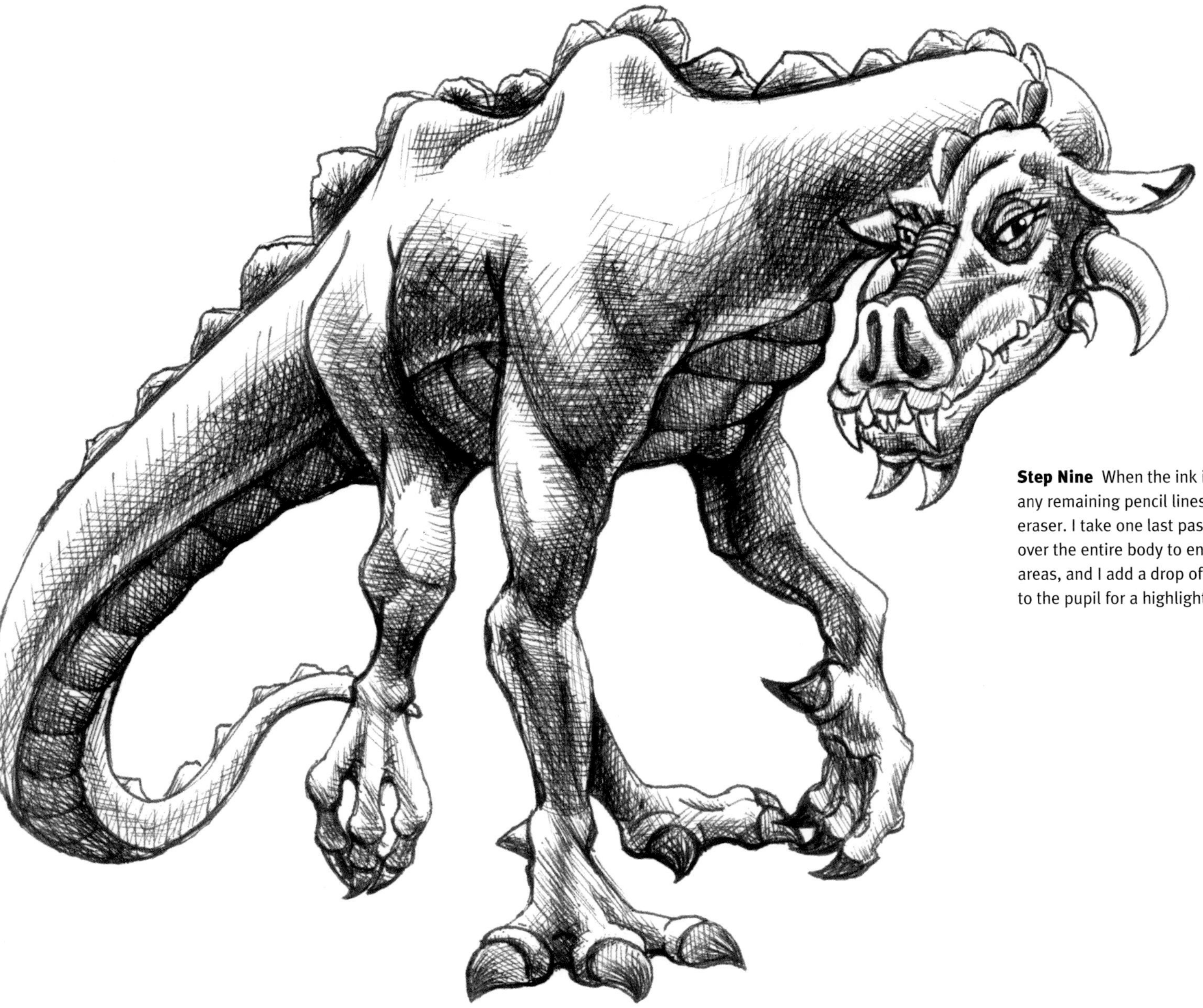

Step Nine When the ink is dry, I erase any remaining pencil lines with an art gum eraser. I take one last pass of hatching over the entire body to enrich the darkest areas, and I add a drop of correction fluid to the pupil for a highlight.

Hydra

A hydra is a many-headed dragon. It can have as few as seven or as many as one million heads! The hydra has notoriously bad breath because it exhales poison or acid. This monster often inhabits rivers.

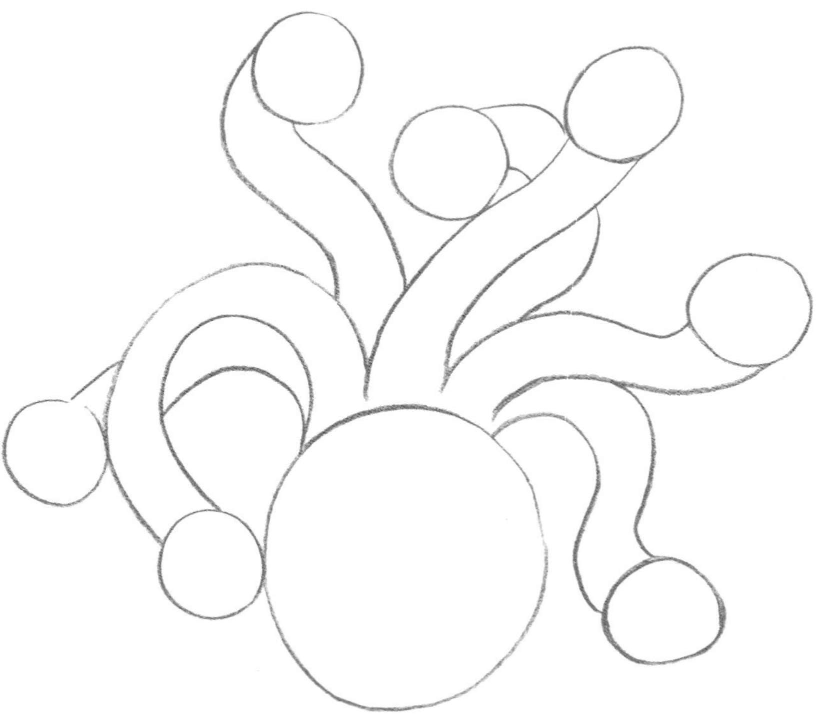

Step One I start by using a 2H pencil to draw the basic shape of the hydra. My main concern in this step is to make sure all these darn heads can exist in the same place in a plausible way!

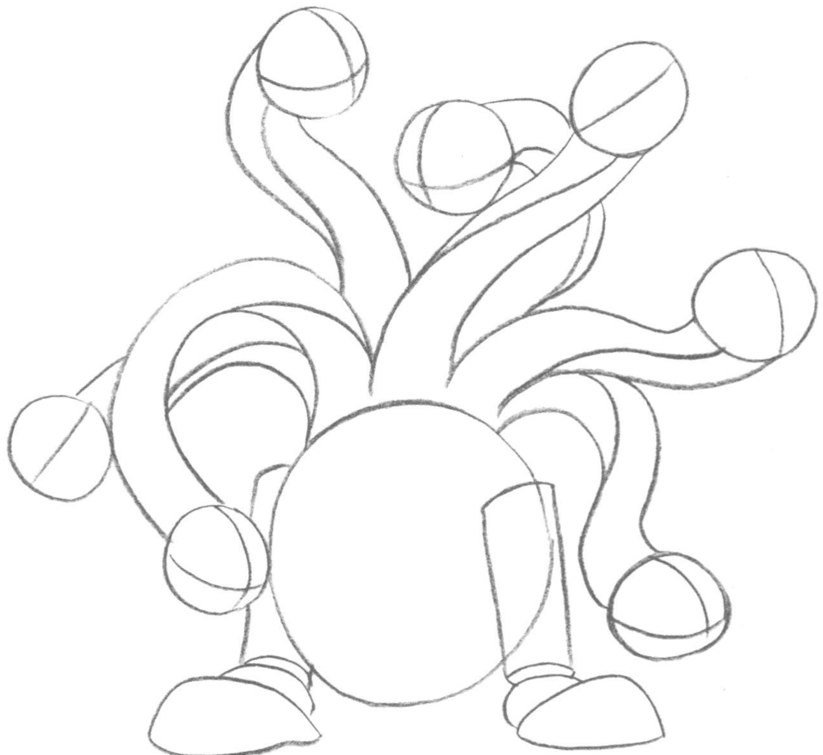

Step Two I draw the legs and feet, which at this point look like a robot's. Then I continue building the shapes, adding facial guidelines to the heads. I also delineate the fronts of the necks with lateral lines.

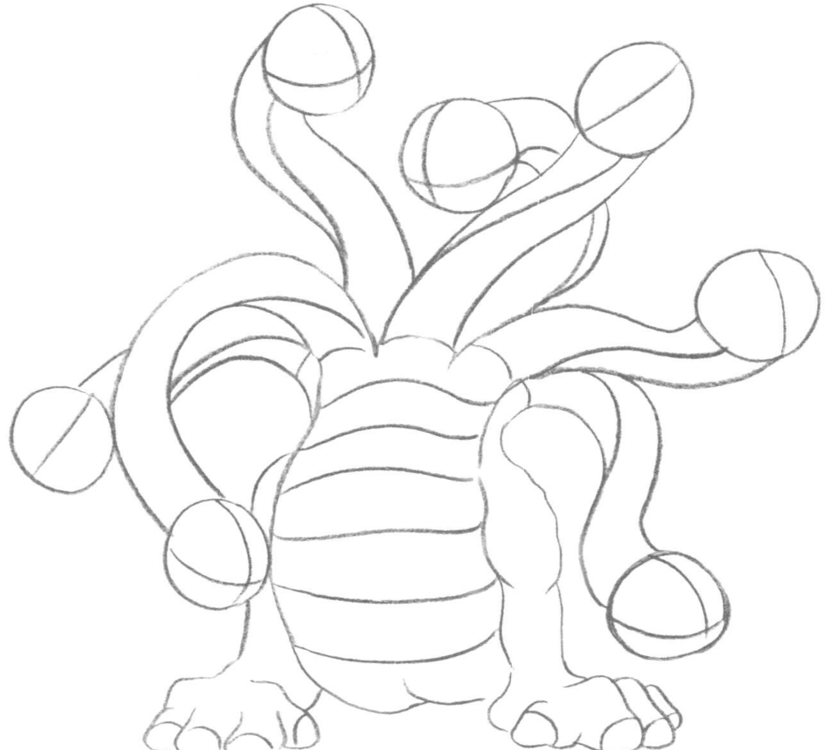

Step Three Using my construction lines, I refine the legs and feet. I make the feet a cross between a human's and an elephant's, with large, squarish nails. Then I add horizontal lines on the torso that curve with the body's form.

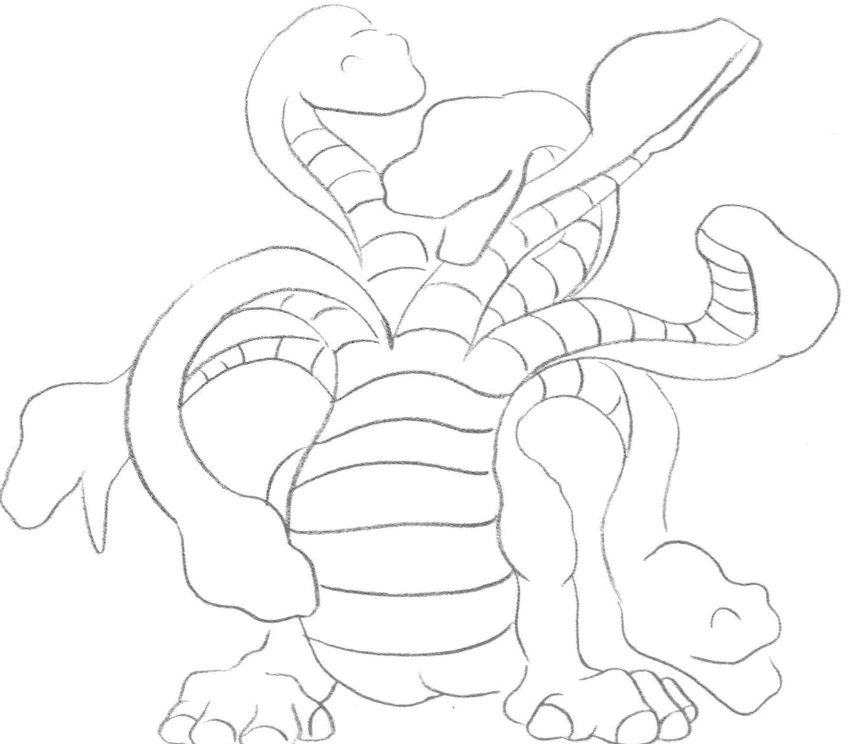

Step Four I continue the curved lines up the fronts of the necks, refining the heads as I go and erasing my construction lines as I no longer need them. These heads are quite rounded, rather than angular—they remind me of baby dinosaurs.

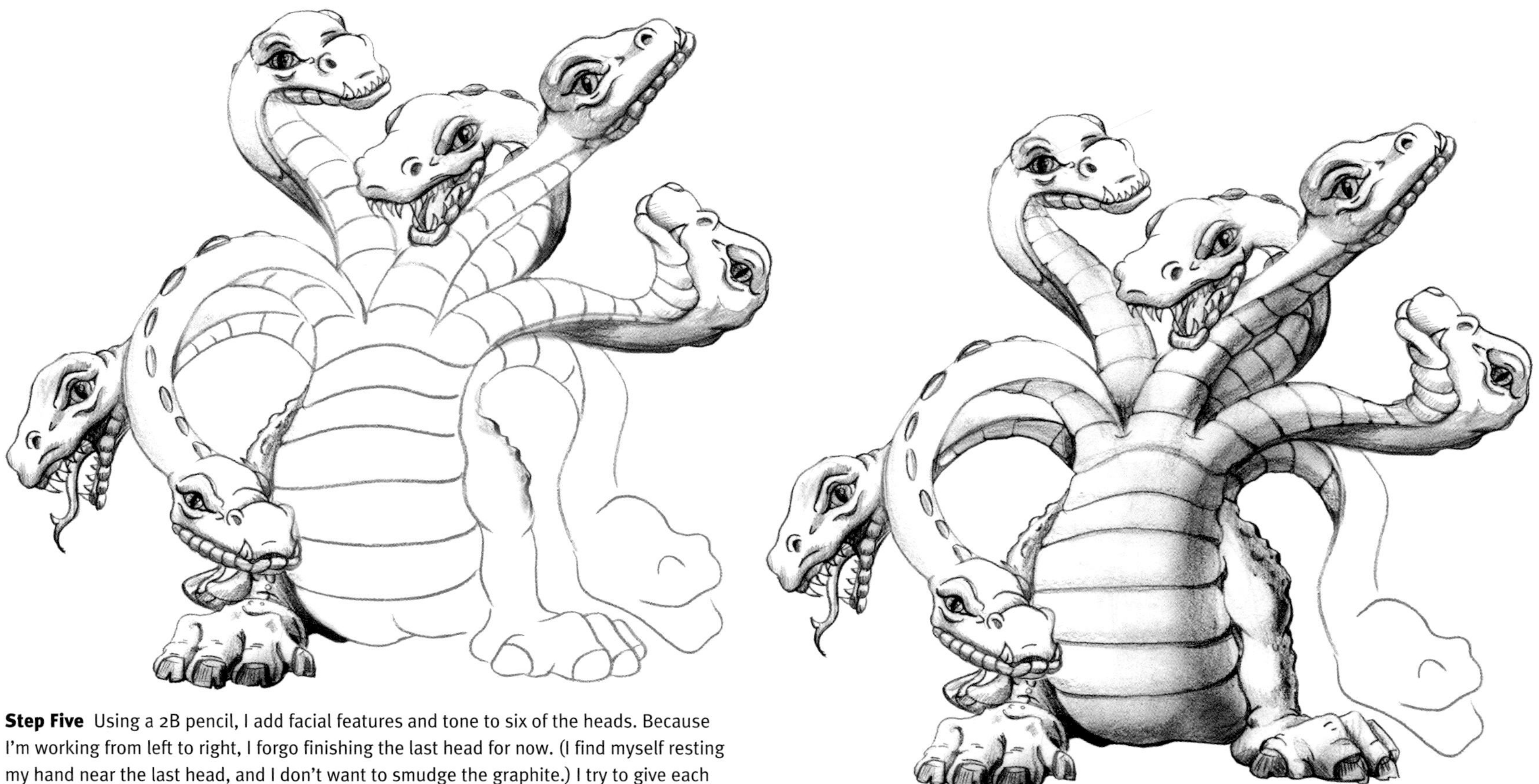

Step Five Using a 2B pencil, I add facial features and tone to six of the heads. Because I'm working from left to right, I forgo finishing the last head for now. (I find myself resting my hand near the last head, and I don't want to smudge the graphite.) I try to give each head a different personality while maintaining general uniformity, so I vary their poses and features. When adding tone to the heads, I lightly rub the graphite with a paper towel to create a simple gradation. I draw ridges on some of the necks, and then I move to the creature's haunches, where I add a rough, bumpy texture. I continue this texture down the creature's right leg and onto its foot. I add small circles to enhance the texture, and I draw very unkempt toenails.

Step Six As I continue to build up the overall tone with the soft graphite, I make sure not to grind it into the paper so that I can blend the tone later. Then I shift my attention to the belly scales, shading them and blending with a paper towel. I continue the bumpy texture down the creature's left leg and apply the same ragged-toenail treatment to the creature's left foot.

Step Seven Now I'm ready to render the final head. After doing so, I use a paper towel to blend heavy areas of graphite, creating dark, rich, even tones. I run a vinyl eraser along the contour edges to clean up any stray marks. I also use the eraser to pull out highlights; I use a craft knife to carve specialty shapes in my eraser so I can reach tight areas.

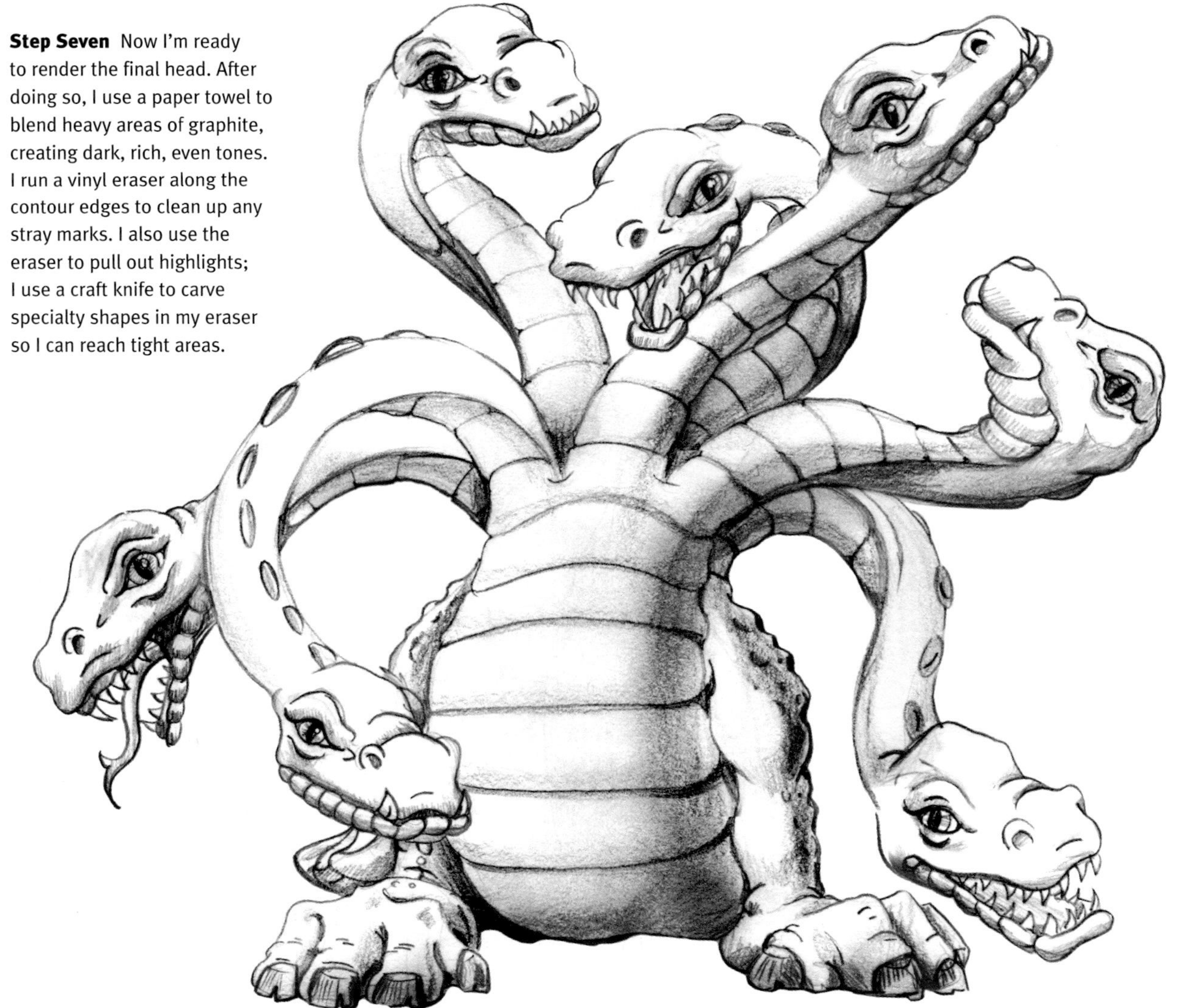

Did you know?

- Greek hero Heracles killed a hydra as one of his Twelve Labors, performed to satisfy the Oracle.
- A hydra is born with seven heads, but each time one head is severed, two heads grow in its place!
- In Greek mythology, the Hydra guarded one of the entrances to the underworld.
- The only way to kill a hydra is to cut off its heads and sear the necks with fire before new heads can grow.

Amphisbaena

An amphisbaena is a two-headed, ant-eating serpent. This warm-blooded reptile can travel quickly by grabbing one set of jaws in the other and rolling like a hoop. Amphisbaena skin will cure colds and can help lumberjacks cut down trees!

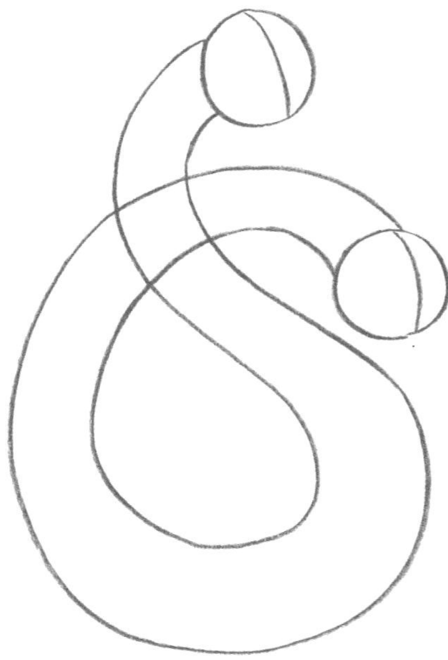

Step One Using a 2H pencil, I lightly sketch the shape of the dragon. I add two circular heads and draw vertical guidelines on both.

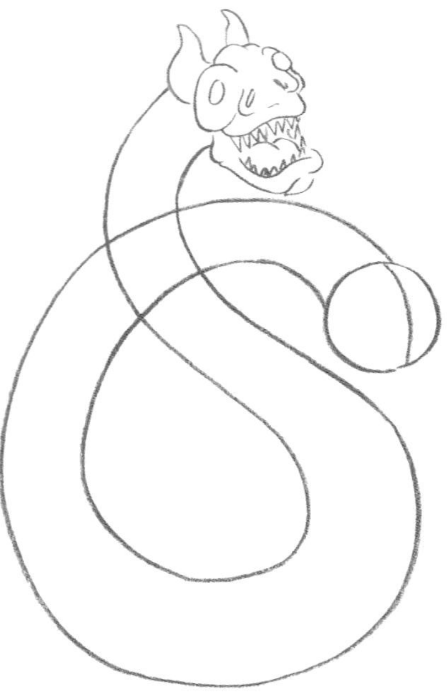

Step Two I begin drawing the features of the upper head, using the vertical line from step one as a guide. I add two thick horns; one donut-shaped and one button-shaped eye; a wide nose; and an open, tooth-filled mouth. I also indicate the tongue.

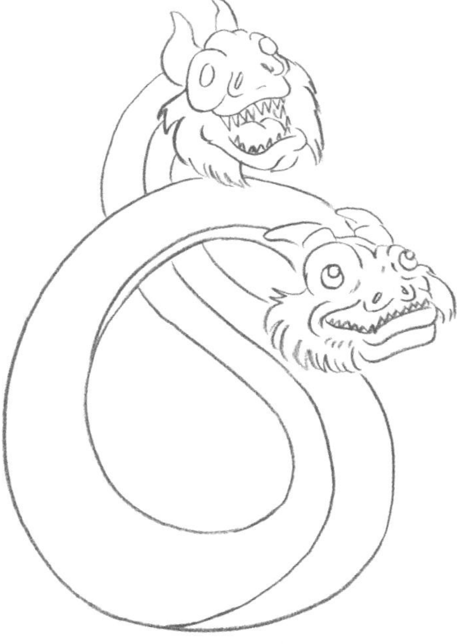

Step Three After adding tufts of hair to the upper head, I begin drawing the lower head. I draw similar features, except this head has its mouth closed, its horns lie flat on its head, and its eyes look up. Then I draw a curving line down the body to differentiate the front from the back.

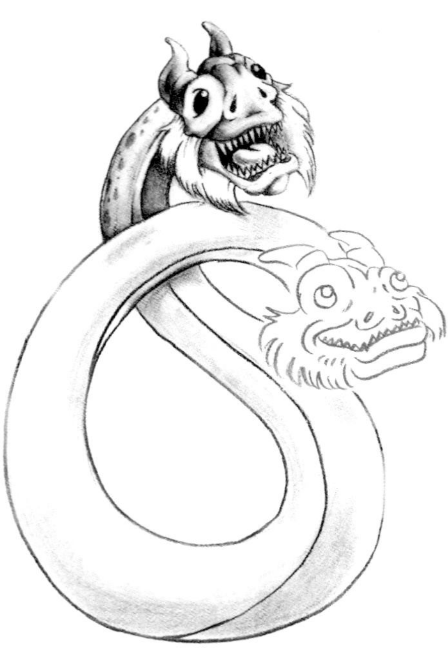

Step Four Using vine charcoal, I begin adding soft, dark tone to the upper head's horns and neck, as well as to the underside of the belly and the area where the upper head's chin casts a shadow on the lower head's neck. Then I use a medium-black charcoal pencil to darken the eyes, nostrils, and inside of the mouth. I pull out a highlight in the pupil with a kneaded eraser. Then I use the charcoal pencil to add spots to the upper head's neck.

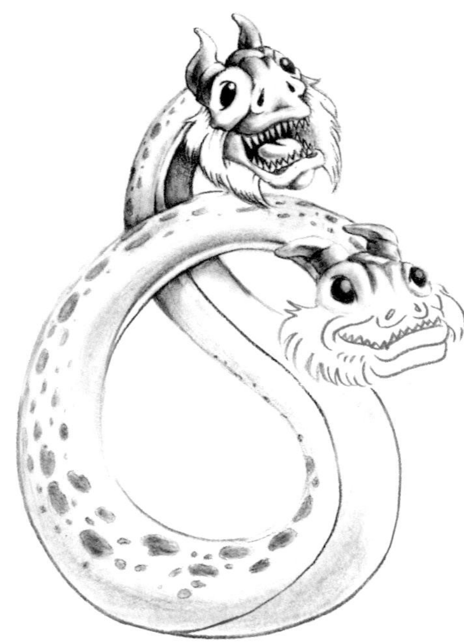

Step Five Switching back to vine charcoal, I continue adding tone to the lower head, softly blending the tone with my finger. (Charcoal smudges easily, so it is especially important to avoid resting your hand on the drawing.) Next I darken the lower head's eyes with the charcoal pencil, and I continue the spot pattern down the rest of the body.

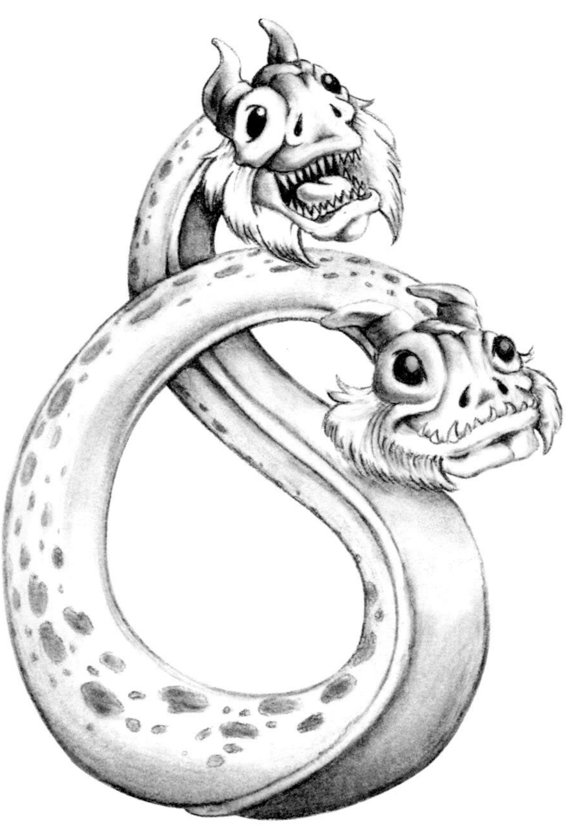

Step Six As I finish building tone on the lower head, I also introduce darker tones to the underside of the belly. I use a craft knife to fashion a fine point on my charcoal pencil and carefully darken the sections that warrant it. Lastly, I go in with a kneaded eraser and pull out more highlights.

Amphitere

Lacking both arms and legs, an amphitere is a plumed, winged serpent. Admired for its beautiful coloration, the amphitere has a hypnotic gaze. If you plant an amphitere's fangs in soil, your very own loyal army will emerge from the ground.

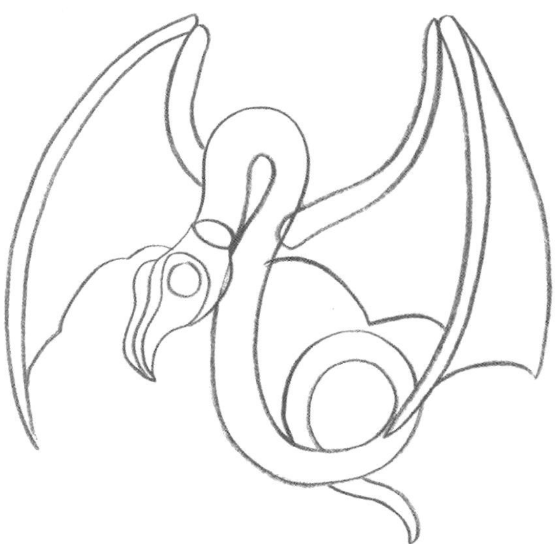

Step One I rough in the general body shapes with a 2H pencil. The wings are large and batlike, the body is slim and serpentine, and the head is birdlike.

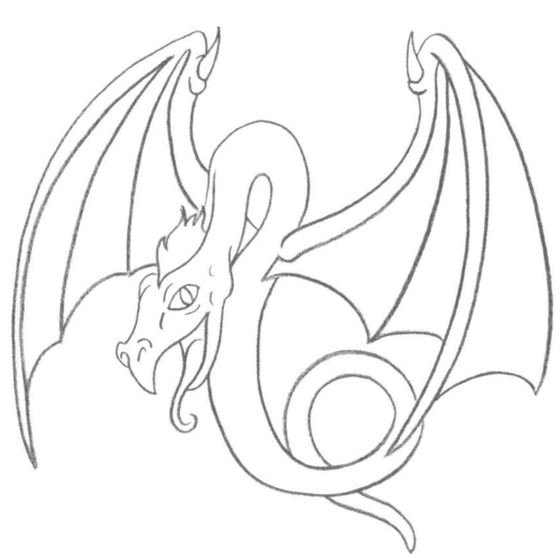

Step Two Still using my 2H pencil, I establish more of the dragon's contours, erasing construction lines as I work. I draw the eye, nose, and mouth, and I add a long, curling tongue.

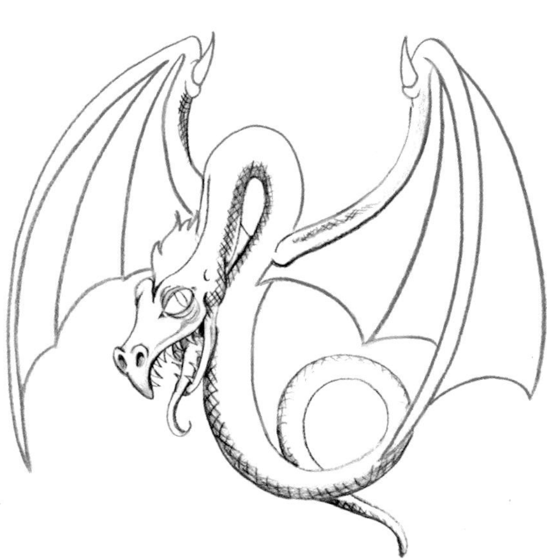

Step Three On the head, I use my 2B pencil to refine the features and shade the nostrils and the inside of the mouth. I add the sharp teeth and draw the tuft of hair. Next I define the wings, adding sharp spikes to the tips. Then I establish a simple crosshatch pattern for the scales on the body. I keep the scales confined to areas of shadow, or along exterior contour lines. Because the 2B is soft, I can blend by lightly rubbing my finger over the scales.

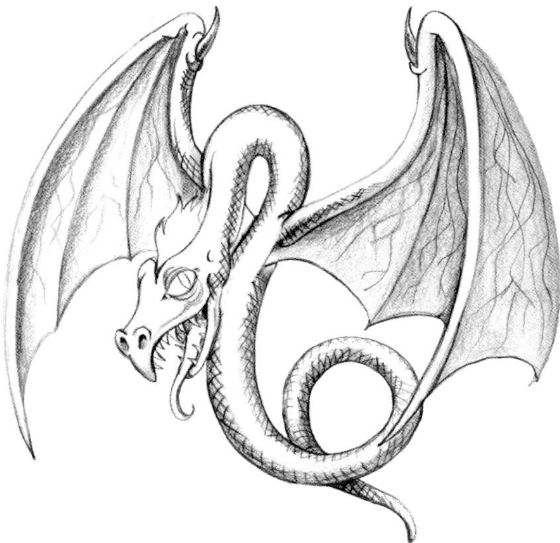

Step Four I finish crosshatching the body before turning my attention to the wings. I make sure my 2B pencil has a rounded, soft point; then I draw the light, squiggly veins.

Step Five I go back and darken the areas that need it, like the pupil, the wing joints, and the overlapping body parts. Then I add a pointed tip to the tail.

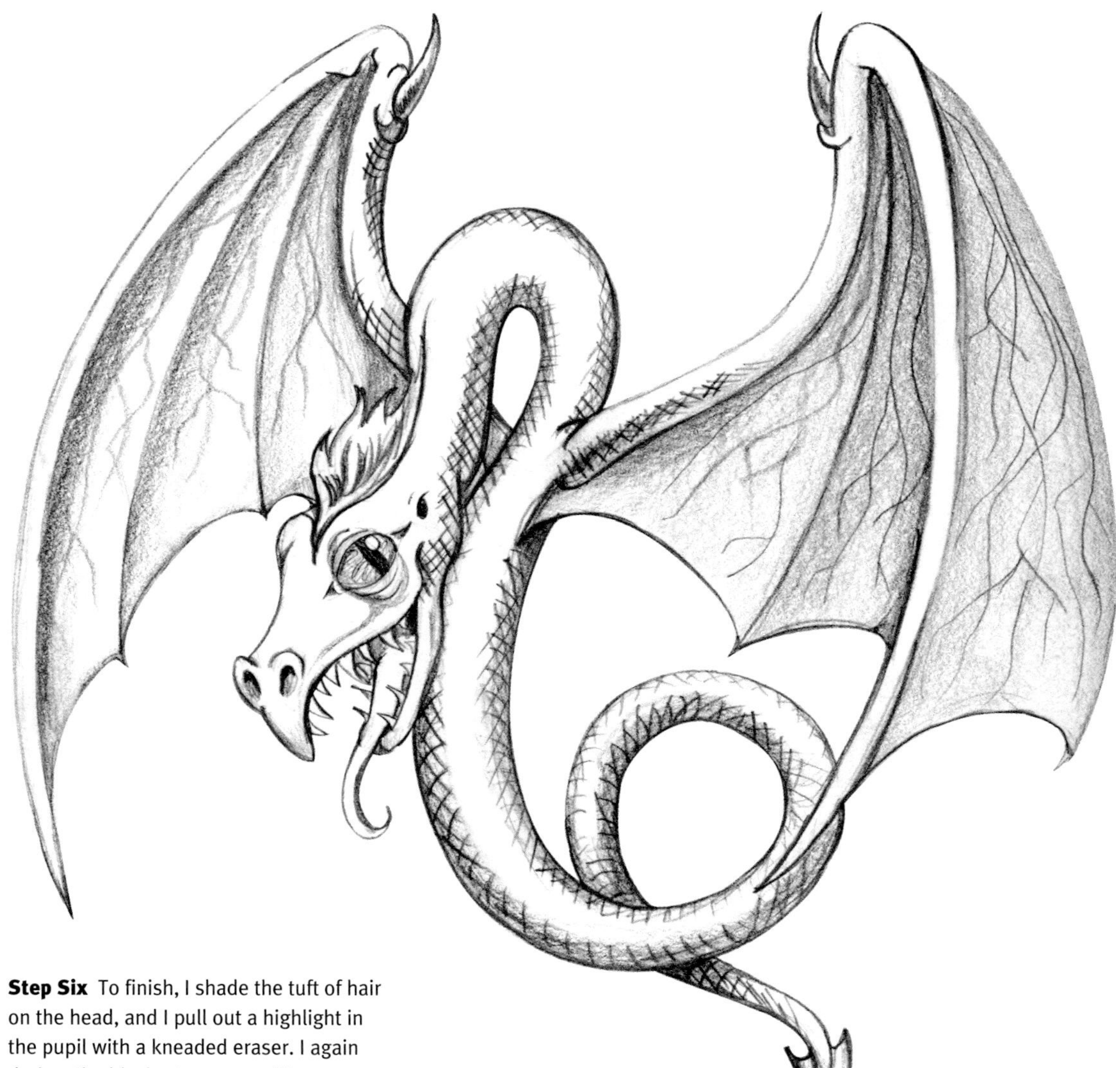

Step Six To finish, I shade the tuft of hair on the head, and I pull out a highlight in the pupil with a kneaded eraser. I again darken the blackest areas, making sure my pencil has a sharp point so I can get into small areas and draw fine details.

Lindworm

A lindworm is an armless dragon with legs and wings. A large creature known for eating cattle, the lindworm was recognized by ancient Europeans as a symbol of war. Despite having wings, this beast generally does not fly.

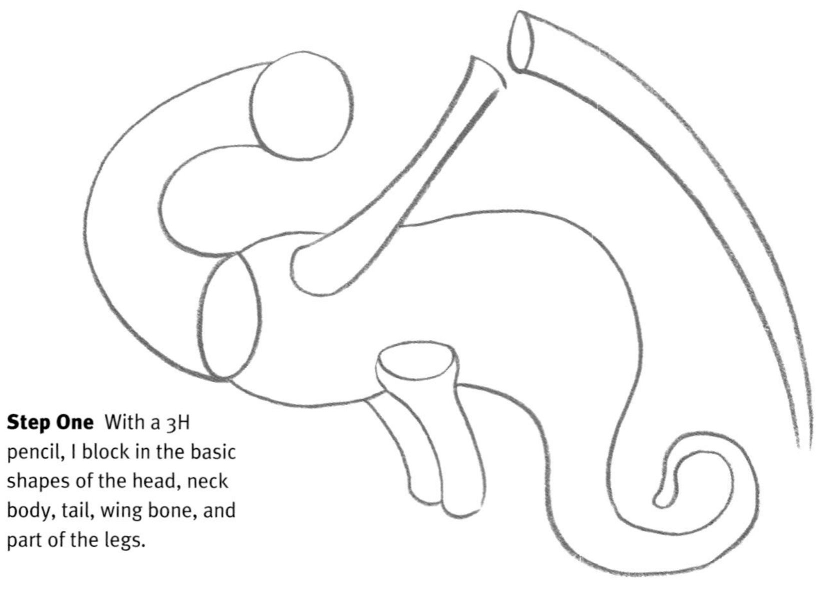

Step One With a 3H pencil, I block in the basic shapes of the head, neck body, tail, wing bone, and part of the legs.

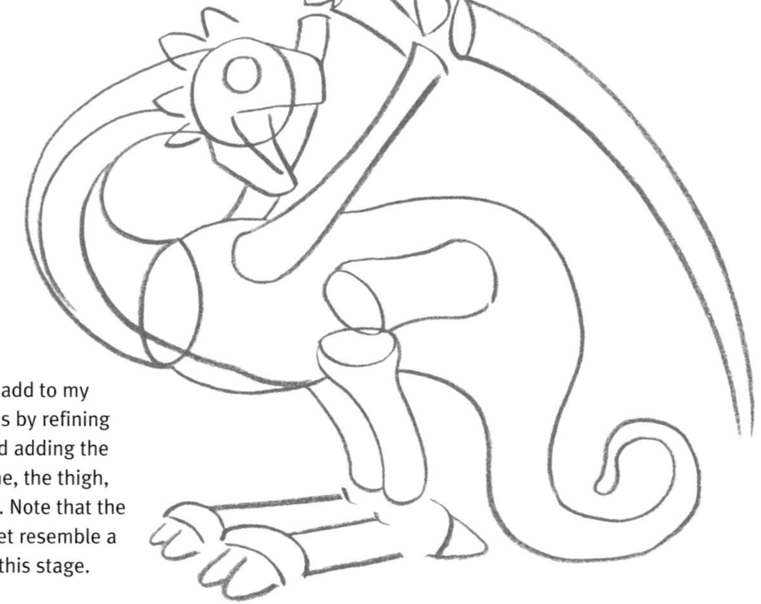

Step Two I add to my initial shapes by refining the head and adding the far wing bone, the thigh, and the feet. Note that the head and feet resemble a rooster's at this stage.

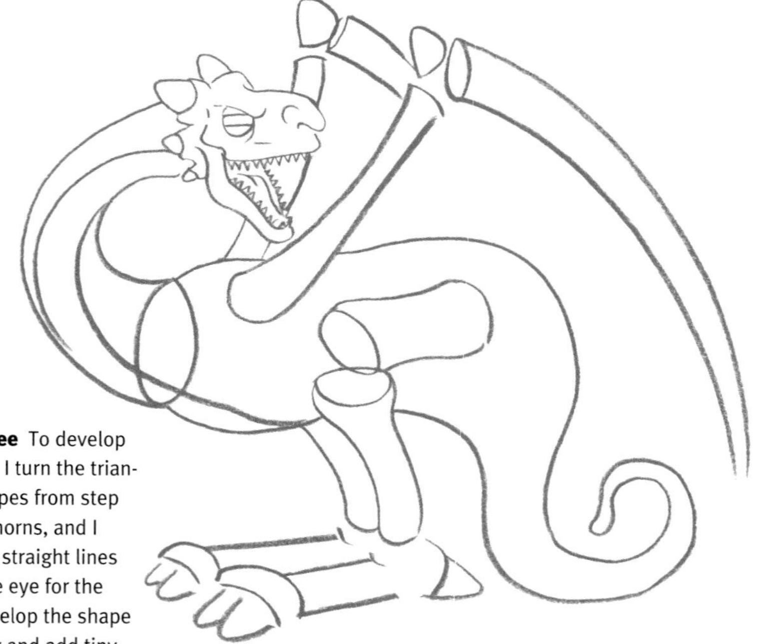

Step Three To develop the head, I turn the triangular shapes from step two into horns, and I draw two straight lines within the eye for the lids. I develop the shape of the jaw and add tiny, sharp teeth and the tongue. Then I add the nose.

Step Four Using my basic shapes, I refine the neck, body, and legs. The legs are thin, while the feet are oversized and the thigh is muscular. I draw the large, birdlike wing that overlaps the tail, and I add the spikes at the tips of the wings, erasing guidelines as I draw.

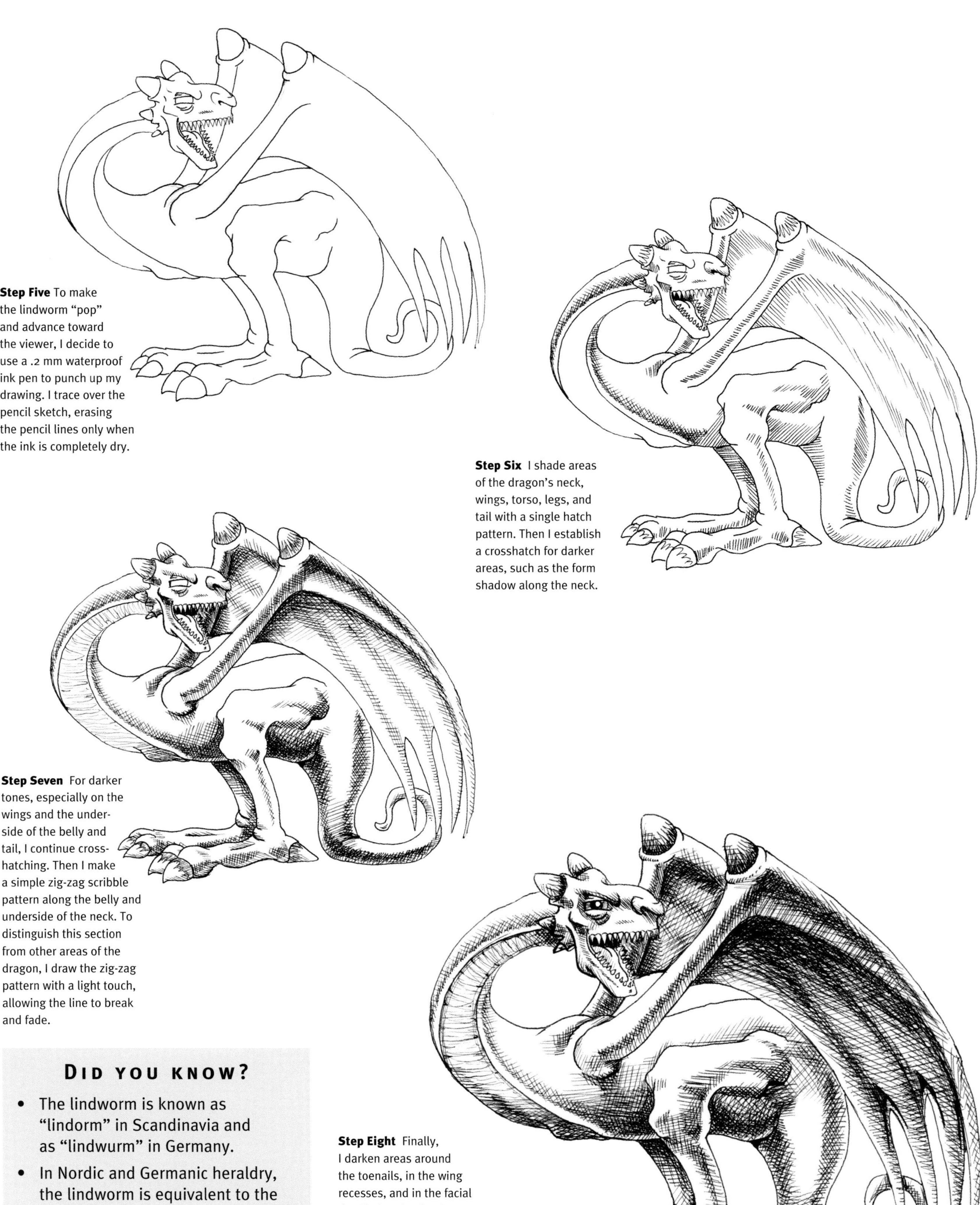

Step Five To make the lindworm "pop" and advance toward the viewer, I decide to use a .2 mm waterproof ink pen to punch up my drawing. I trace over the pencil sketch, erasing the pencil lines only when the ink is completely dry.

Step Six I shade areas of the dragon's neck, wings, torso, legs, and tail with a single hatch pattern. Then I establish a crosshatch for darker areas, such as the form shadow along the neck.

Step Seven For darker tones, especially on the wings and the underside of the belly and tail, I continue crosshatching. Then I make a simple zig-zag scribble pattern along the belly and underside of the neck. To distinguish this section from other areas of the dragon, I draw the zig-zag pattern with a light touch, allowing the line to break and fade.

Step Eight Finally, I darken areas around the toenails, in the wing recesses, and in the facial details. I make the tips of the wings pure black. Then I darken the hatching along the bottom of the feet, inside the wings, and along the underbelly.

Did you know?

- The lindworm is known as "lindorm" in Scandinavia and as "lindwurm" in Germany.
- In Nordic and Germanic heraldry, the lindworm is equivalent to the wyvern.
- The lindworm often is depicted without wings.

Wyvern

Related to the lindworm, the wyvern is a carnivorous, energetic beast that usually possesses two legs, batlike wings, and a barbed tail. It does not have arms. This creature was popular as a heraldic icon in the medieval period.

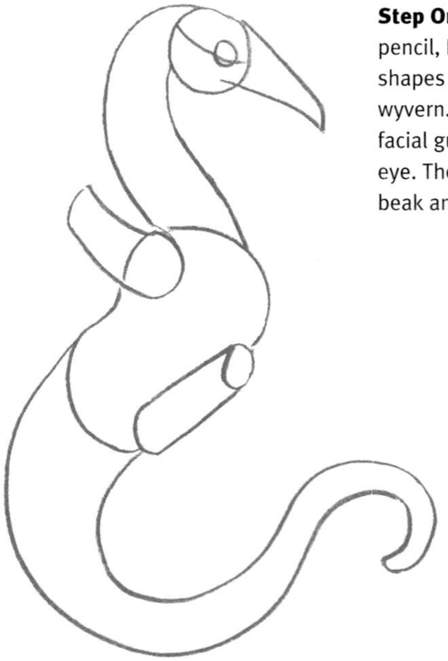

Step One With a 3H pencil, I sketch the basic shapes that make up the wyvern. Using a horizontal facial guideline, I place the eye. Then I draw a pointed beak and a whiplike tail.

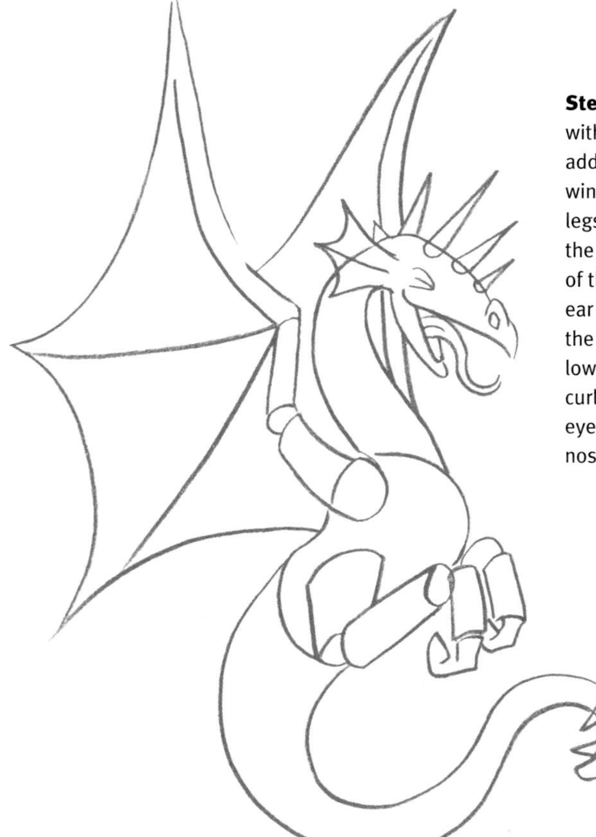

Step Two Continuing with the basic shapes, I add two large, angular wings, a pair of curled legs, and spikes along the head and at the end of the tail. I add a finlike ear that is reminiscent of the wings. Then I draw the lower jaw, adding a long, curled tongue. I refine the eye a bit and add a large nostril.

Step Three Focusing on the head, I extend the eye and add small, sharp teeth. I change the shape of the tongue a bit and give it a forked tip. I refine the spikes on top of the head, adding ridges where they protrude from the head. Then I refine the ear a bit.

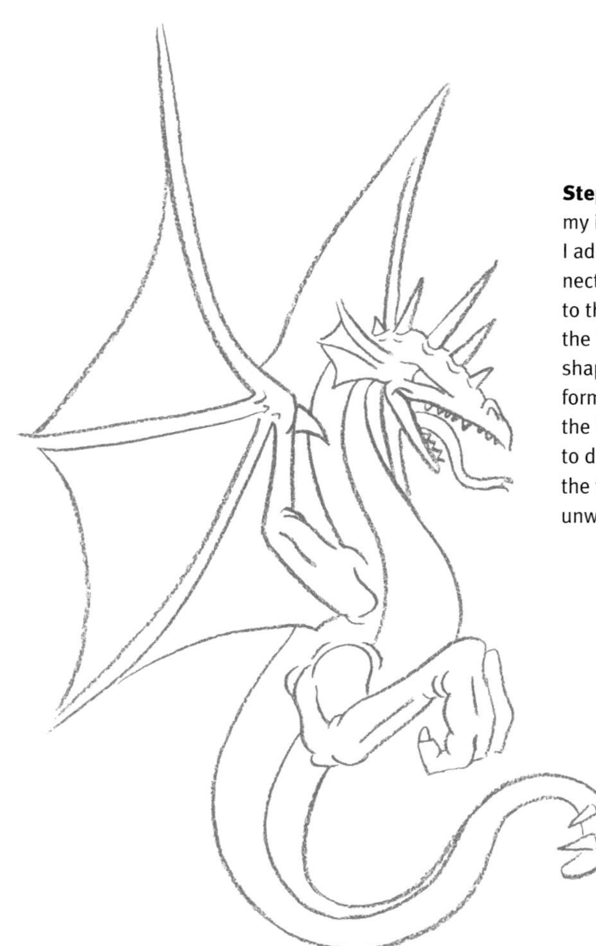

Step Four Building on my initial wing structures, I add definition and connect the base of the wing to the body. Then I refine the legs, using the basic shapes to create their forms. I add a claw to the foot, then draw a line to delineate the front of the tail. Next I erase any unwanted lines.

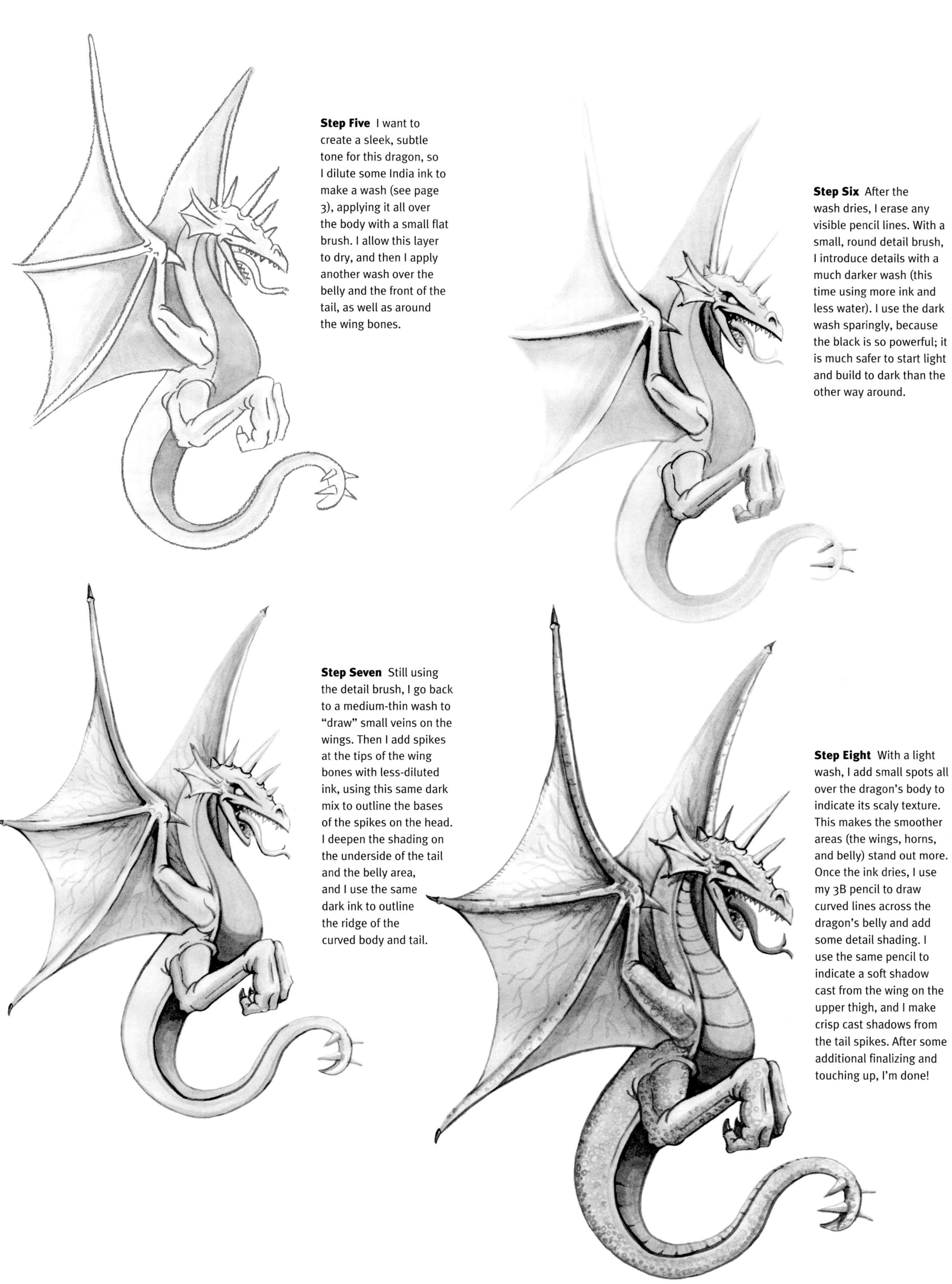

Step Five I want to create a sleek, subtle tone for this dragon, so I dilute some India ink to make a wash (see page 3), applying it all over the body with a small flat brush. I allow this layer to dry, and then I apply another wash over the belly and the front of the tail, as well as around the wing bones.

Step Six After the wash dries, I erase any visible pencil lines. With a small, round detail brush, I introduce details with a much darker wash (this time using more ink and less water). I use the dark wash sparingly, because the black is so powerful; it is much safer to start light and build to dark than the other way around.

Step Seven Still using the detail brush, I go back to a medium-thin wash to "draw" small veins on the wings. Then I add spikes at the tips of the wing bones with less-diluted ink, using this same dark mix to outline the bases of the spikes on the head. I deepen the shading on the underside of the tail and the belly area, and I use the same dark ink to outline the ridge of the curved body and tail.

Step Eight With a light wash, I add small spots all over the dragon's body to indicate its scaly texture. This makes the smoother areas (the wings, horns, and belly) stand out more. Once the ink dries, I use my 3B pencil to draw curved lines across the dragon's belly and add some detail shading. I use the same pencil to indicate a soft shadow cast from the wing on the upper thigh, and I make crisp cast shadows from the tail spikes. After some additional finalizing and touching up, I'm done!

Western Dragon

Dragons originating in Western mythology have four legs, long necks, a thick body, and batlike wings, which don't grow until adulthood. The traditional meal for a Western dragon is a sheep, an ox, or a human—consumed monthly. The Western dragon usually is a malevolent, fire-breathing creature that lives underground and hoards treasure.

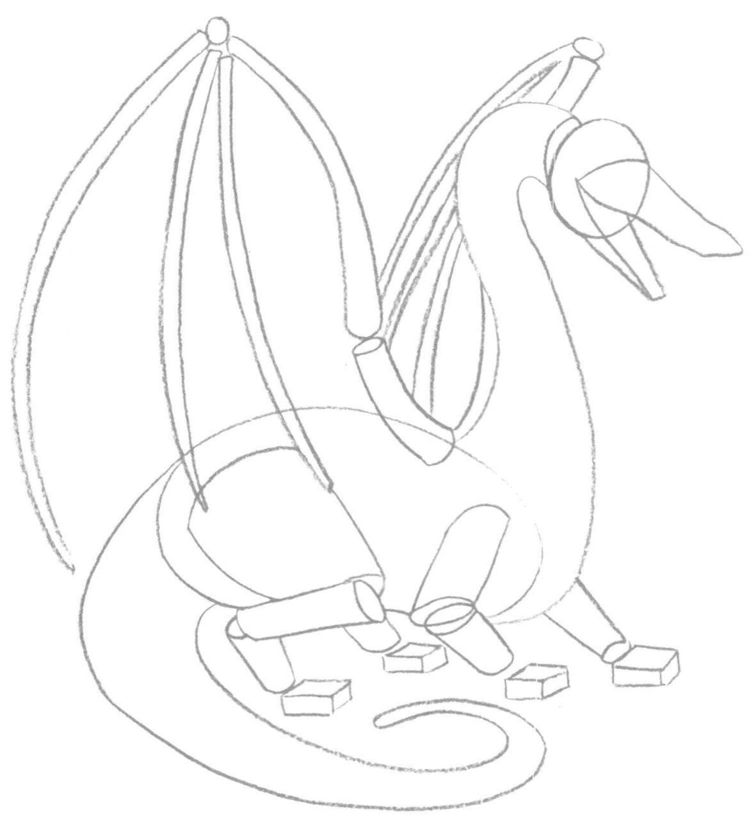

Step One I start by using a 2H pencil to construct my dragon-to-be with simple shapes, such as cylinders, cubes, and cones. This helps me understand how these individual parts exist in real space and interact with one another.

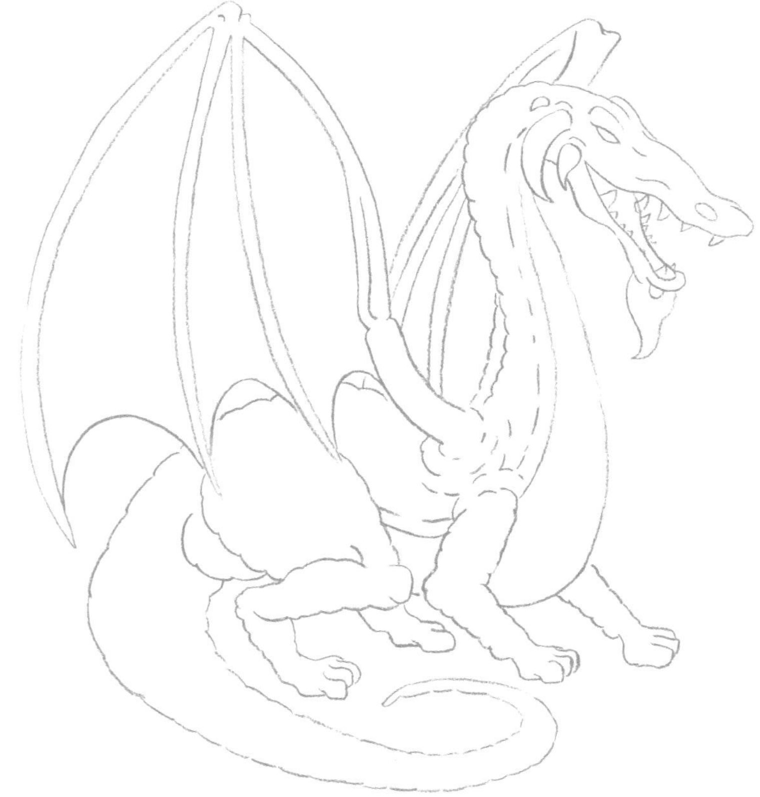

Step Two I develop the contour lines around the basic shapes with my 2H pencil. I add the eye, teeth, beard, and horns to the crocodile-like head. When I'm happy with my basic drawing, I erase the construction lines.

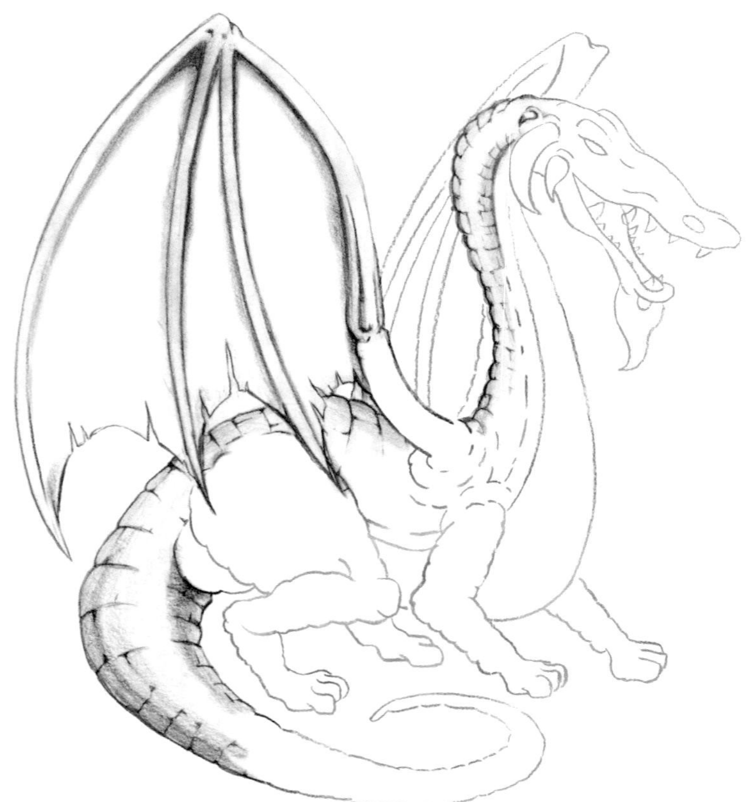

Step Three Jumping in with my 2B pencil, I begin the tonal rendering. I want to establish two textures right away—the hard, rough texture of the dragon's skin and the leathery, thin surface of its wings. I use cobblestone as inspiration for the dragon's skin.

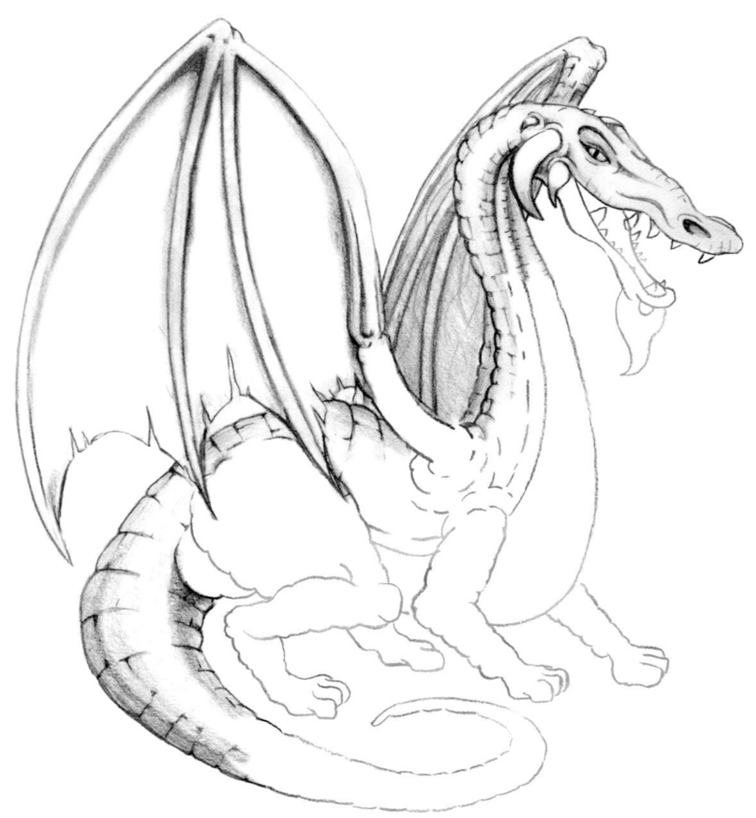

Step Four I darken the far wing to give it a lower contrast and push it back into the picture, providing a sense of distance. Then I shade down the top of the head, detailing the pupil, brow, and nostril. I also go over some of the teeth to darken them.

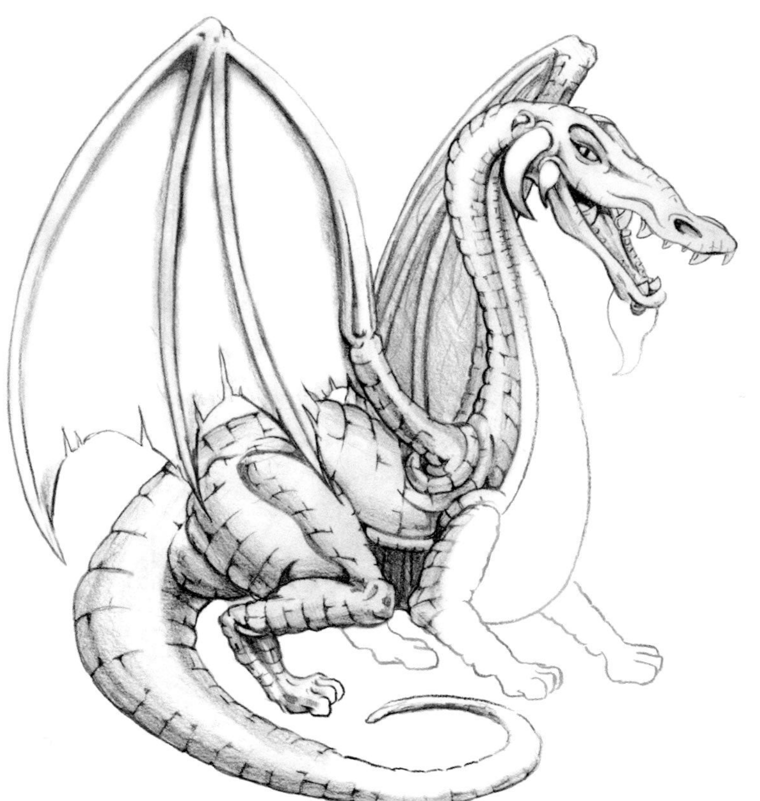

Step Five As I continue to shade the dragon's body, I add "cracked" scales that follow the form of the body. (Notice that the scales are smaller at the end of the tail than they are at the beginning, where the surface is wider.) I shade inside the mouth, making the back of the mouth the darkest area.

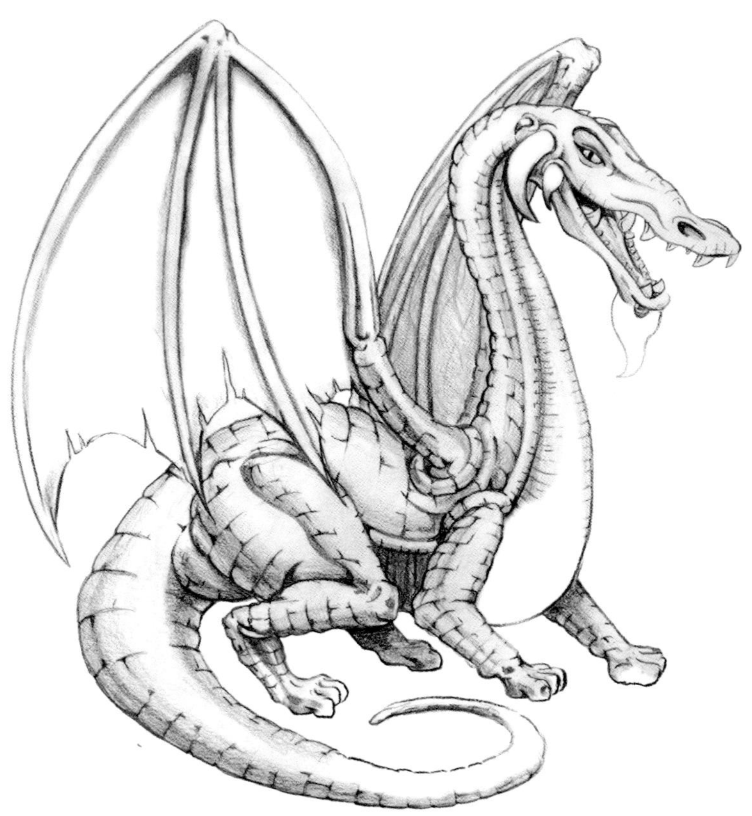

Step Six I shade the rest of the dragon's body, except the belly. I draw short horizontal lines from the top of the neck down toward the belly to indicate ridges. Then I continue the scales down the front legs and refine the lionlike paws.

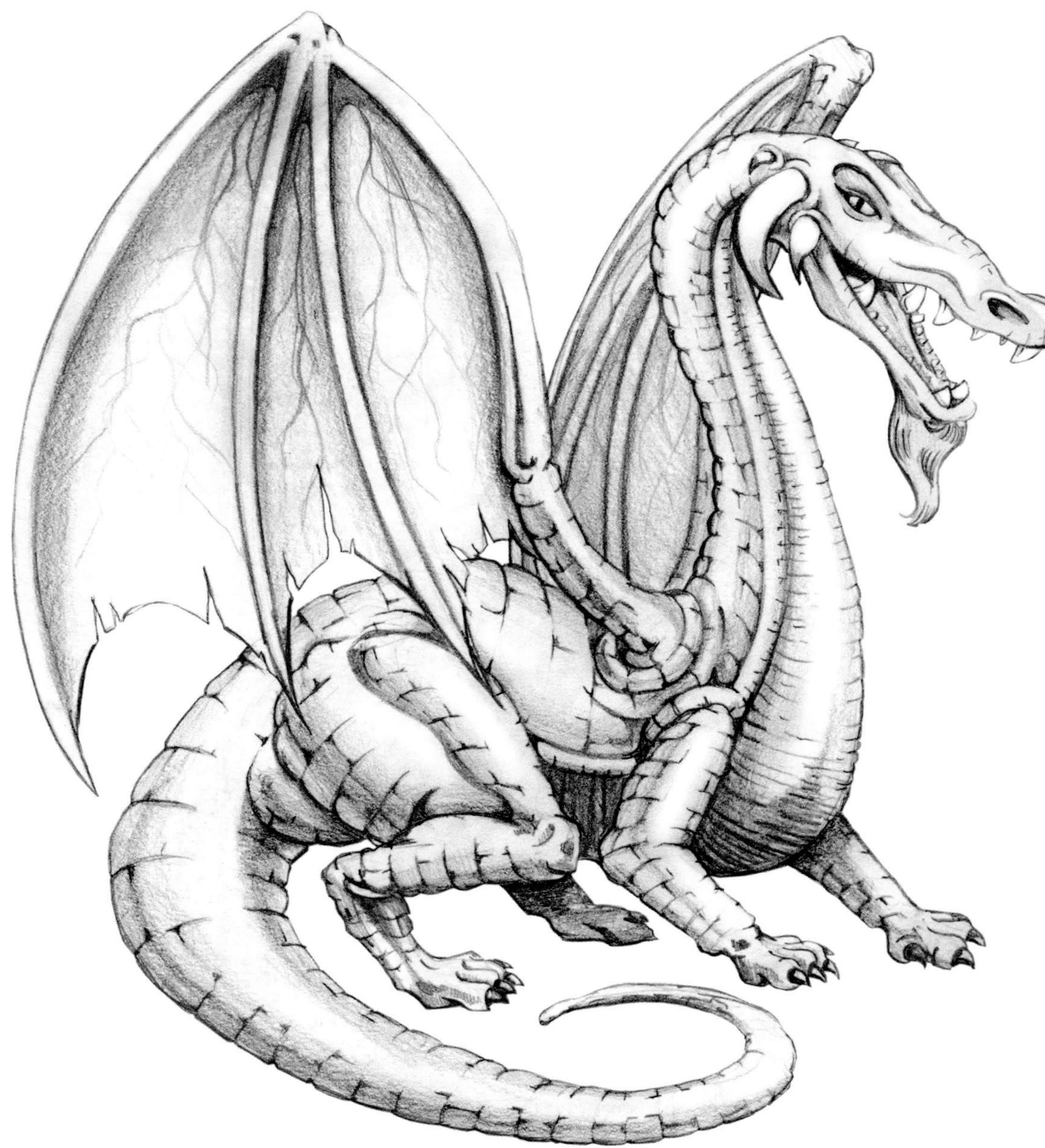

Step Seven I finish shading the front of the dragon, adding more horizontal ridges as I reach the belly. Then I shade inside the wings, creating the veins with a very blunt, rounded 2B pencil; I detail the veins with a very sharp 2B. I draw sharp claws on three of the paws and shade the beard, adding curved lines to show its form. Then I clean up any errant pencil marks with a vinyl eraser; I use the same eraser to lift out highlights on the teeth and horns.

Eastern Dragon

Eastern dragons are described as having a mane of feathers, tiger paws, antlers, eagle claws, carp scales, bull ears, rabbit eyes, and a snake body. Traditionally, most Eastern dragons are water dragons. Many of them lack wings and do not breathe fire. A benevolent creature, the Eastern dragon's power comes from the pearl it holds.

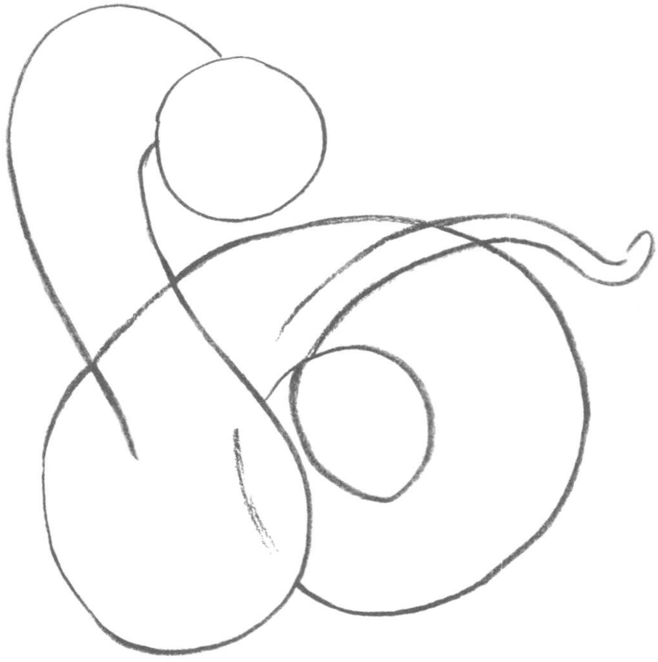

Step One First I use an HB pencil to sketch the body, including the S-shaped neck, the curled torso, and the thin, curved tail.

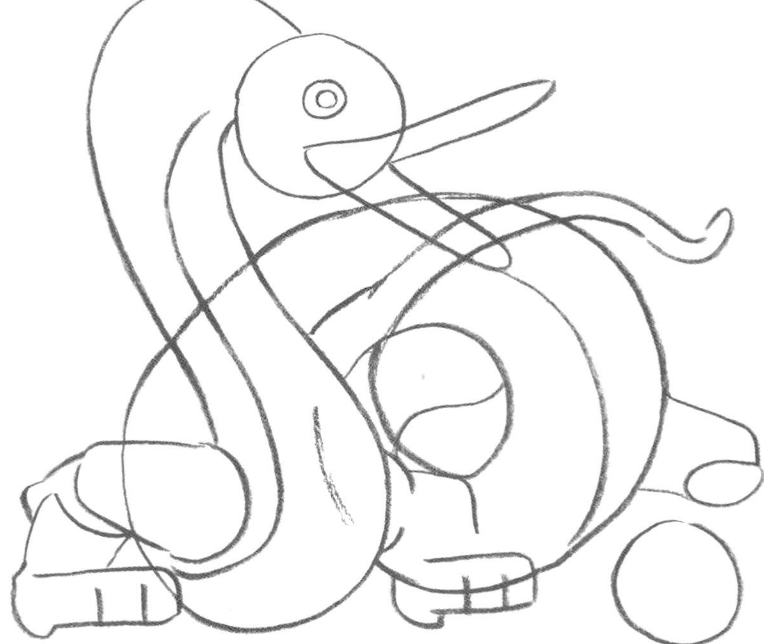

Step Two I add the front legs, feet, mouth, and eye. Then I draw a circle for the pearl. Notice how the beast's head looks like a duck at this stage.

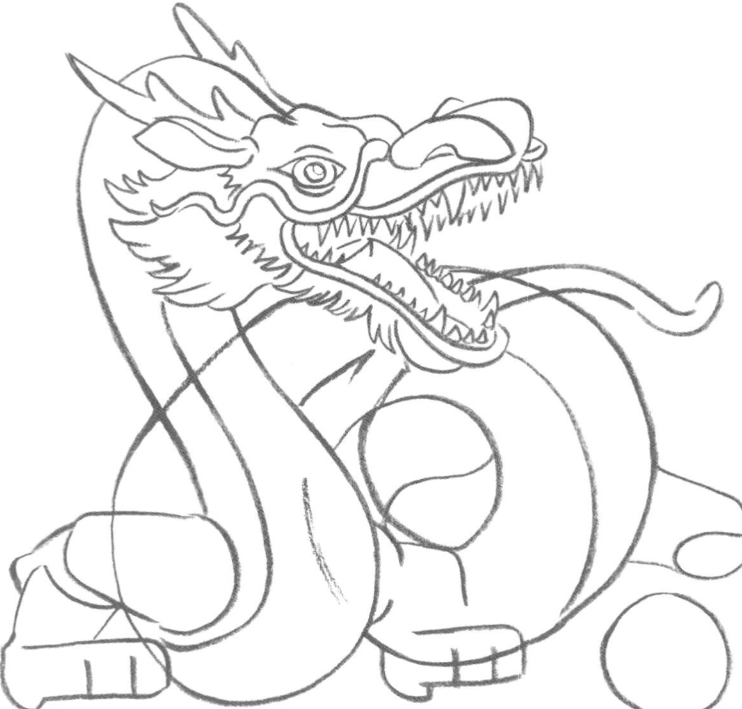

Step Three Turning my attention to the head, I add the details. I draw the antlers at the back of the head, the ear, and the wispy mane on the side of the face. Next I draw the giant nose. I add sharp teeth and a large tongue inside the mouth. I also extend the choppy mane around the mouth, and I add the rest of the details around the nose, eye, and mouth.

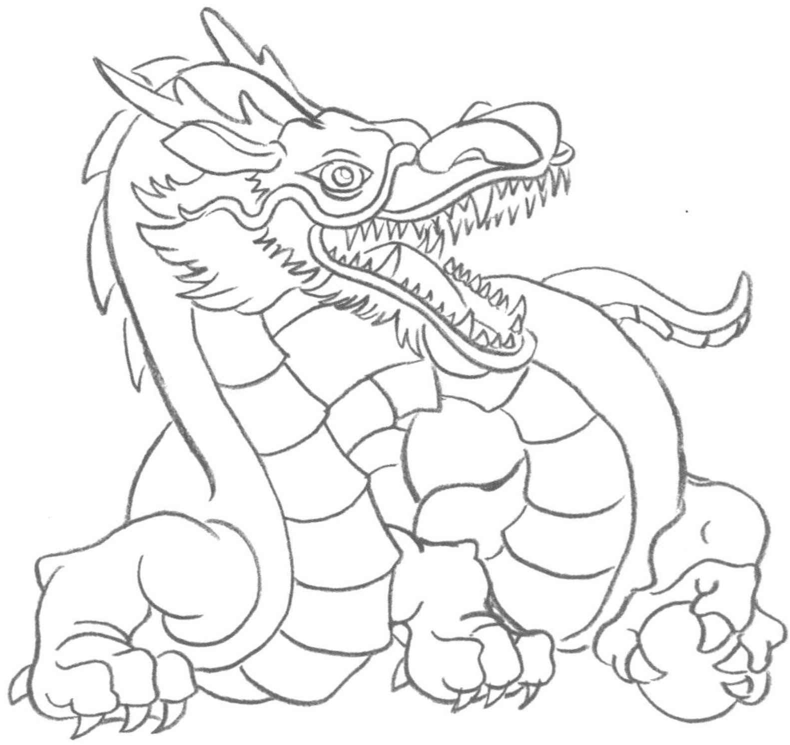

Step Four Using my construction lines, I refine the rest of the body. I make the limbs short and pudgy, adding spikes of skin at the joints. Then I add sharp claws to the feet, and I draw the back foot that grasps the pearl. I add ridges to the dragon's torso and the underside of the tail, and I erase any unnecessary lines.

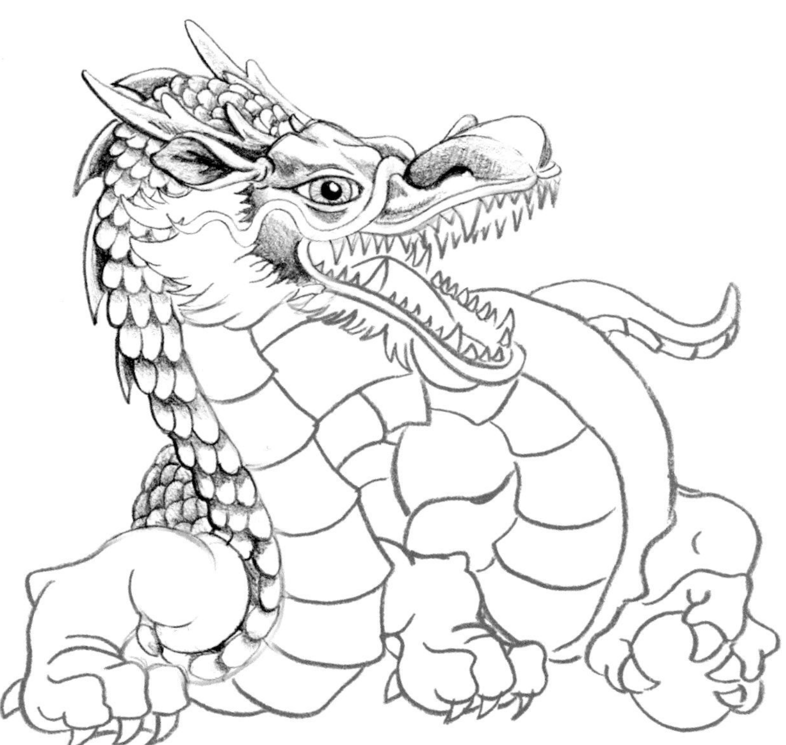

Step Five I draw a scale pattern starting at the back of the head and extending to the dragon's right foreleg. I want the scales to look fishlike, so I use medium-sized U shapes. I begin to create areas of gradation across the scales with a 3B pencil. This pencil is very soft and easily smudged, so I work carefully from left to right (as I am right-handed). Then I move to the face and begin shading the nose, around the eye, and the area near the mane. I also shade the iris and add the dark pupil, leaving a large highlight in the pupil.

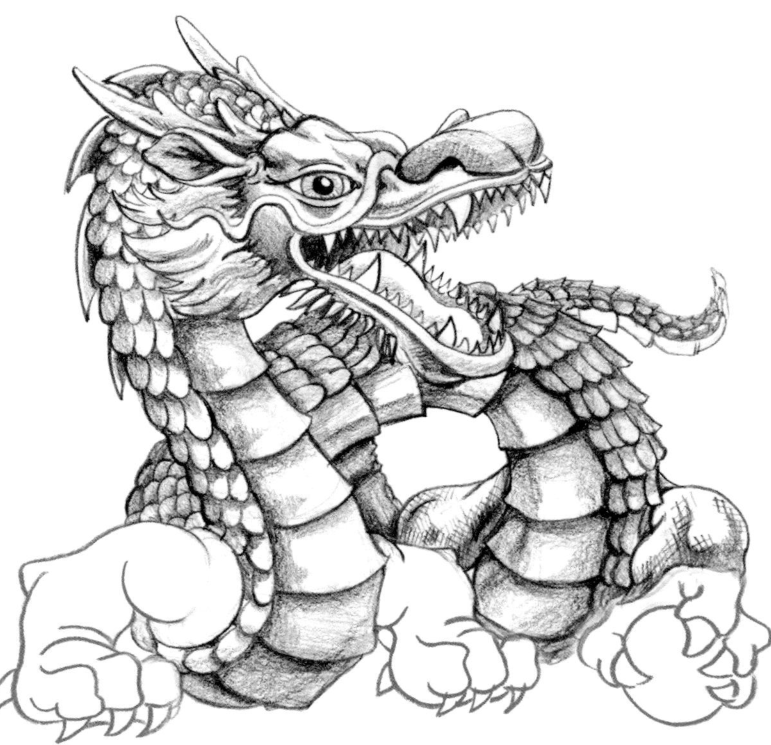

Step Six I continue the scale pattern along the rest of the tail, including the tip. Then I return to the face and shade inside the mouth. I darken the outlines of the teeth, making them more prominent. Next I shade the mane and the scales on the torso and the underside of the tail. I want this area to look shiny, so I leave many highlights.

Did you know?

- Three-toed dragons are Japanese.
- Four-toed dragons are Indonesian.
- Five-toed dragons are Chinese or Korean. (But according to some sources, ordinary Chinese dragons have four toes, whereas imperial dragons have five.)

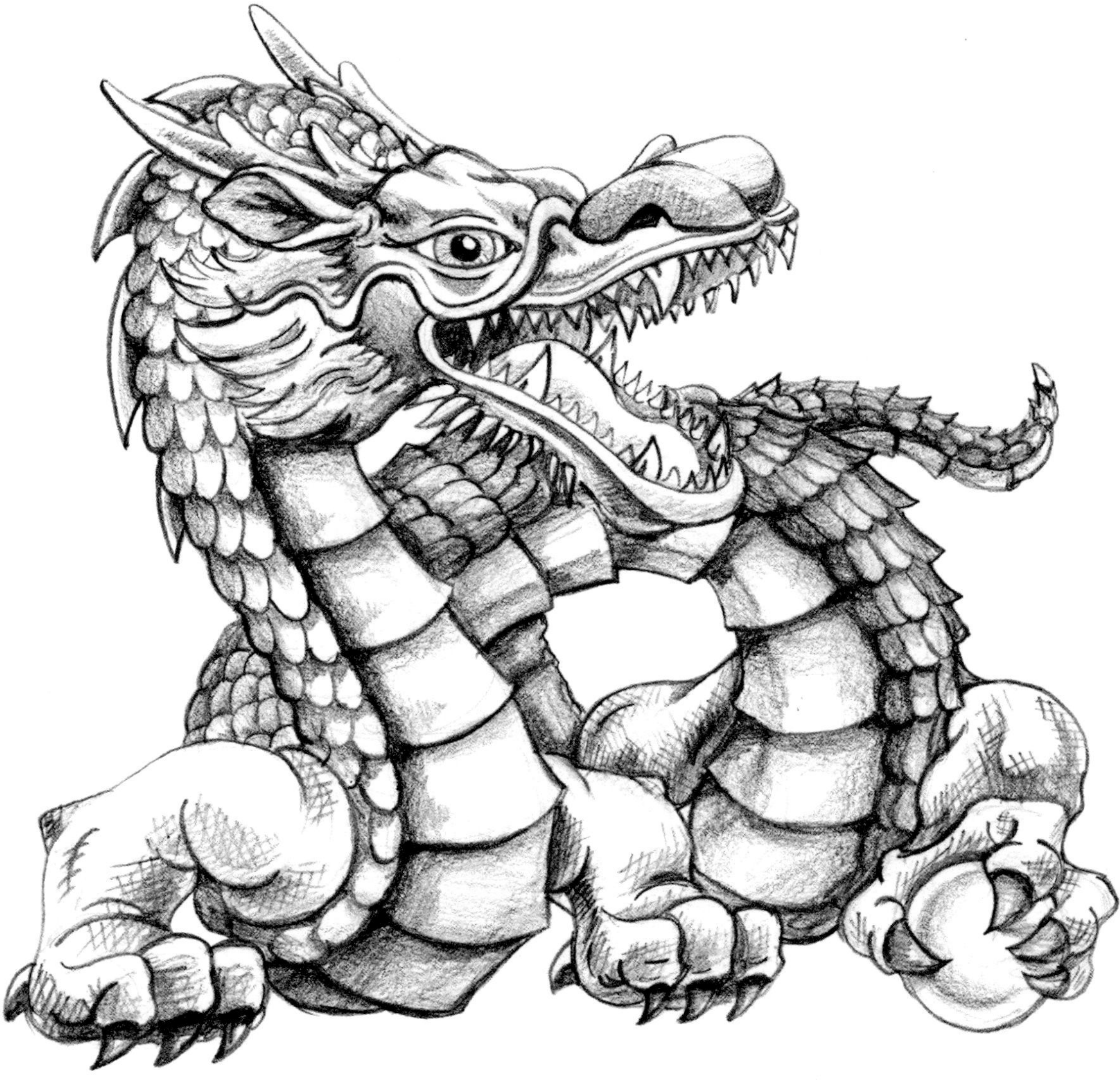

Step Seven To give the dragon an entirely different scale pattern on the limbs, I use a simple crosshatching technique to establish a shiny, low-relief scale pattern. I continue that pattern onto the front limbs. Then I begin to add definition to the pearl. The texture of a pearl is very different from the dragon's scales—I build up tones there very softly, so it looks smooth in comparison with the rough, scaly dragon. Using a vinyl eraser, I remove any stray marks and clean the area around the image. I use a craft knife to carve the eraser so I can work with it in smaller areas. I darken my final tones along the torso, and I fill in the claws, leaving a highlight on each one.

Fafnir

Norse dragon Fafnir was once a dwarf. But soon after he joined forces with his brother Regin to murder their father—the dwarf king Hreidmar—for his treasure, Fafnir decided he didn't want to share his newfound riches. Due to his greed, he was slowly transformed into a dragon. Regin then avenged his brother's selfishness by having his son, Sigurd, slay the dragon.

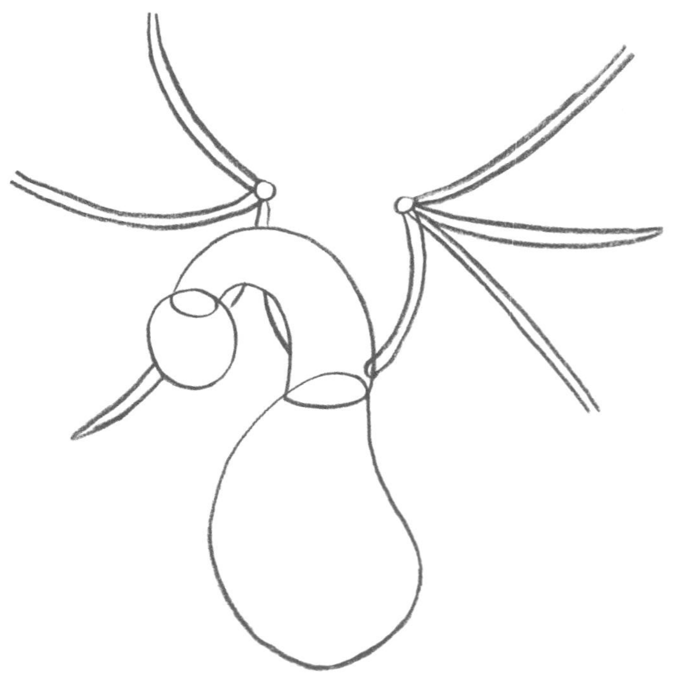

Step One With a 2H pencil, I block in the basic shapes that make up the upper portion of the dragon. I draw a teardrop shape for the torso, a curved cylinder for the neck, and a small circle for the head. Then I use curved shapes that resemble swords for the wing bones.

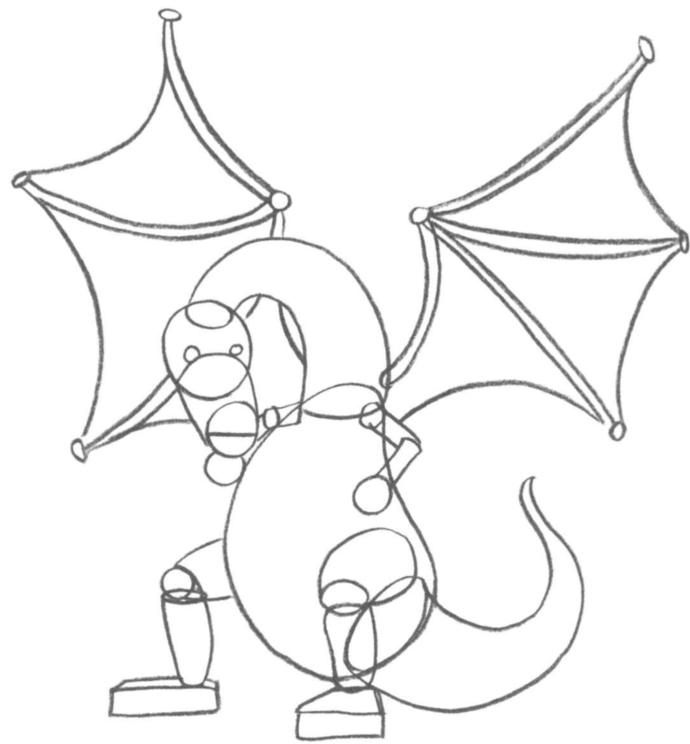

Step Two I connect the bones of the wings with curved lines, adding small circles at the tip of each bone. Then I add the long snout and two beady eyes. I draw circles, boxes, and cylinders to block in the arms and legs, and I draw the thick tail.

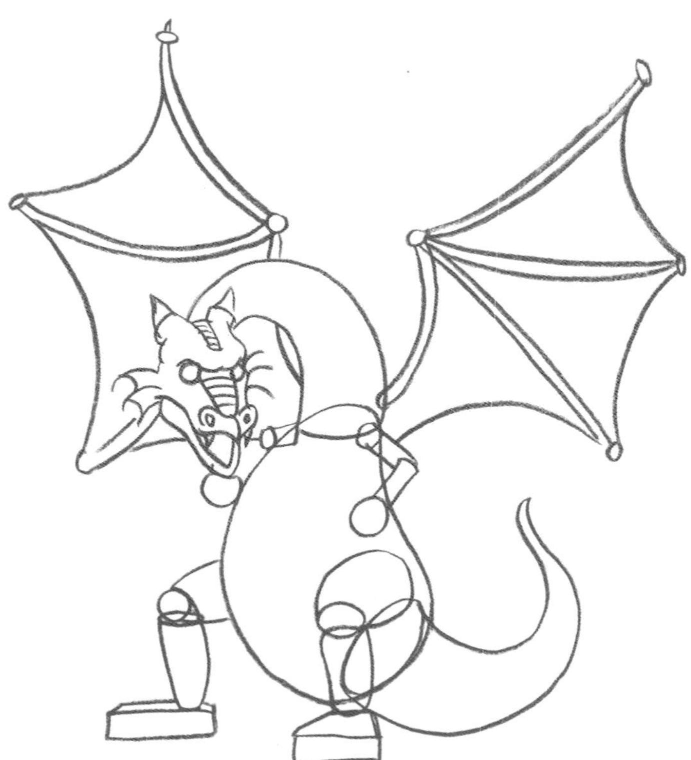

Step Three Now I add some details to the head. I draw the sharp horns, the webbed fins on either side of the face, and the striped pattern that reaches from the top of the head to the forehead and from the eyes to the nose. Then I add the nostrils and the open mouth, suggesting two sharp fangs at the top of the mouth. I use a curved line to indicate the furrowed brow, and then I erase any remaining construction lines on the head.

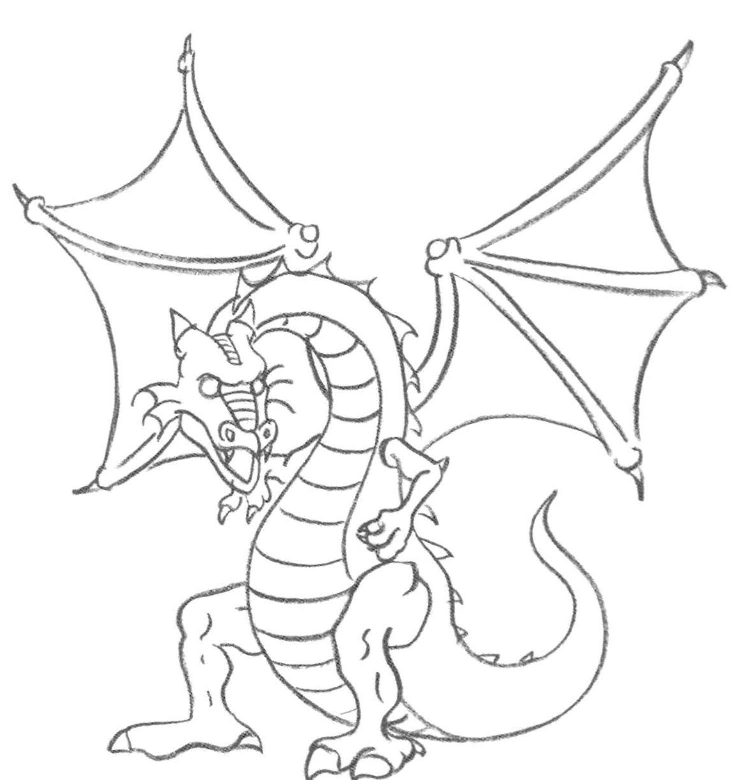

Step Four Using the basic shapes as guides, I develop the arms, legs, hands, and feet. I add sharp claws to the feet and hands, and I draw curved lines to suggest musculature on the legs. The visible elbow gets a spike as well. Then I add the striped scales down the belly and the spikes down the neck and onto the tail. I also refine the wings and add spiked tips to each bone. Then I erase all my remaining construction lines.

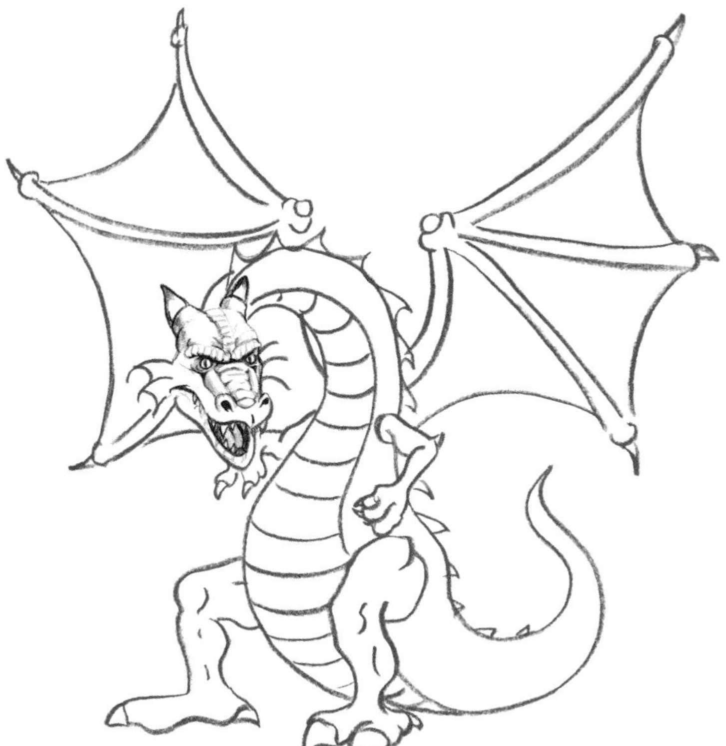

Step Five To achieve darker, softer tones for this dragon, I use a black colored pencil to start rendering the details of the face. I build up the tones slowly, with a soft touch. I work with a small sharpener in hand because the colored pencil is very soft and needs constant resharpening for detailed areas.

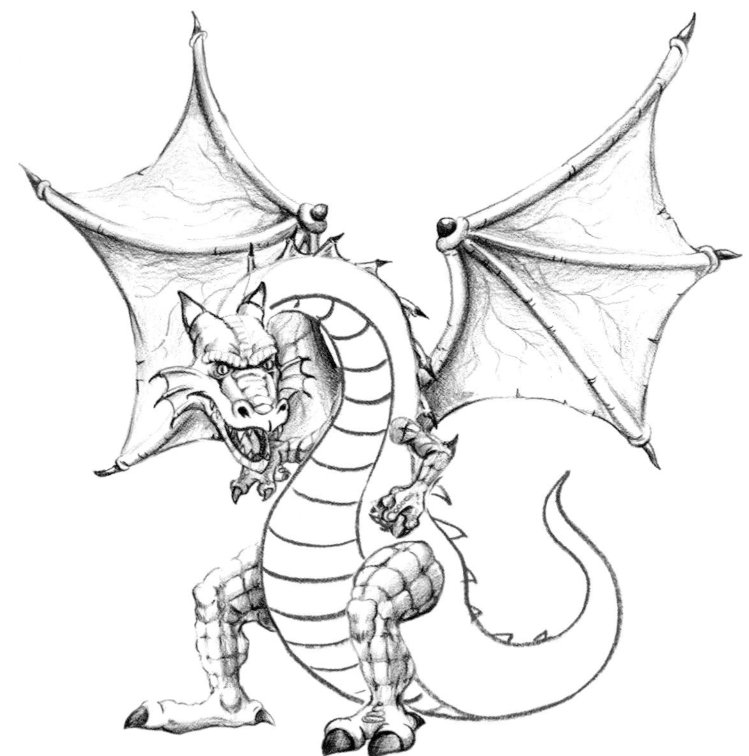

Step Six I use light pressure to shade the wings, placing the darkest tone along the bones and near the neck, where the light is blocked. I also add nicks and tears along the outer edges of the wings, and I darken the tips of the spikes. Then I add very light veins throughout the wings. Next I apply a scale pattern to the legs and arms that reminds me of a quilted mattress. I also add tone to the feet, using the darkest value yet for the claws.

Did you know?

- To slay Fafnir, Sigurd hid in a covered pit and stabbed the dragon as he passed by.
- In a German version of the tale, Fafnir began life as a giant rather than a dwarf.
- After slaying the dragon, Sigurd cooked and tasted Fafnir's heart, gaining the power to understand the language of birds.
- Unbeknownst to Fafnir, the stolen treasure actually was cursed.

Step Seven I continue the scale pattern onto the neck, back, and tail. I prefer working on one section of the body at a time, as it helps me keep the pattern appropriate for the area I'm working on. Once the body scales are complete, I add dark shadows where the scales intersect. Next I shade the wide scales of the belly, leaving the near side lighter to show that the light is coming from the right. I also darken the tips of the spikes along the back, and I add some round knobs to the end of the tail.

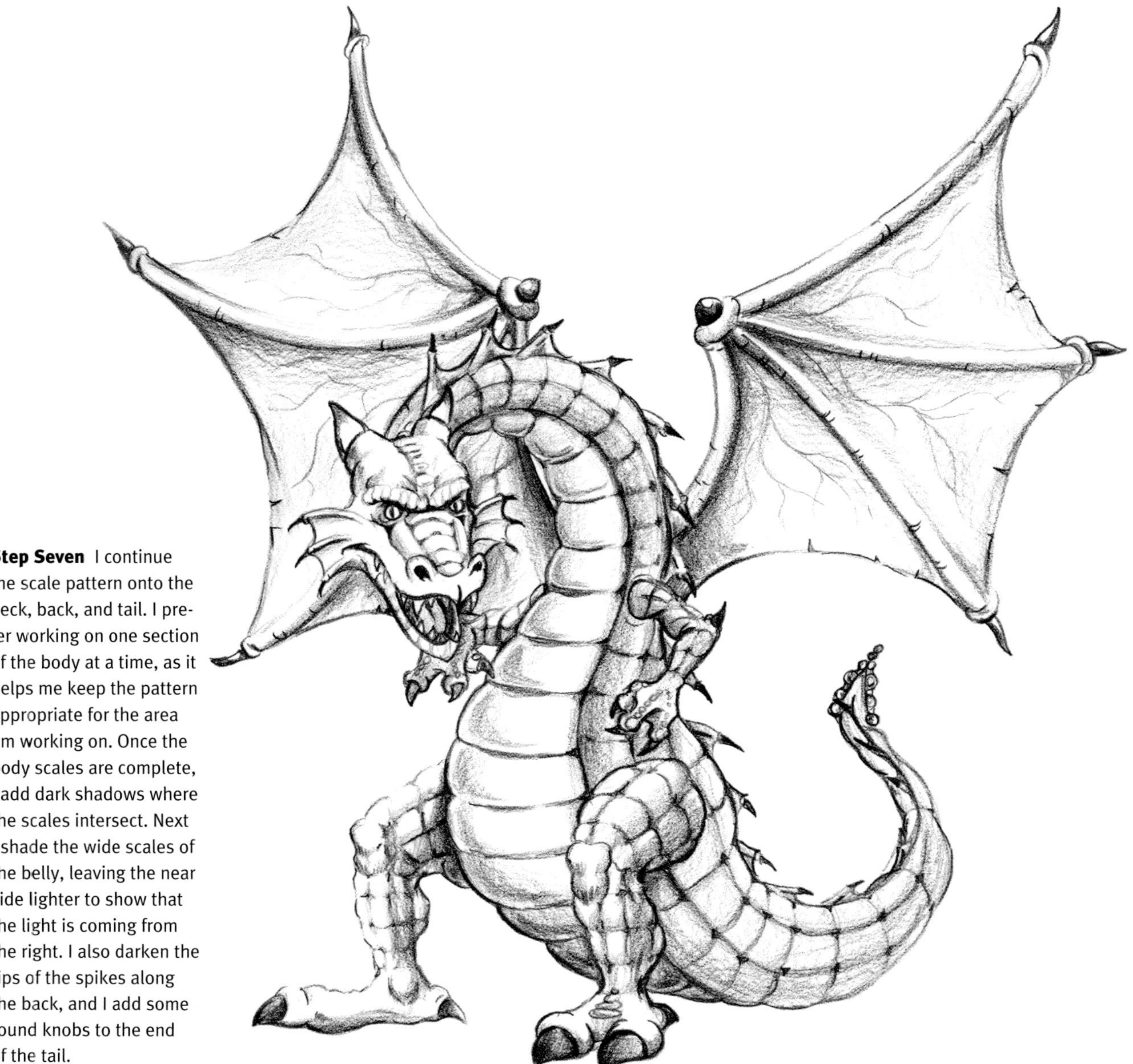

Drachenstein

This wingless firedrake hails from German mythology. The tale comes from the same origin as Fafnir's story—but in this rendition, Drachenstein was born a dragon. He was slain for hoarding a treasure, but it was his own, not ill-gotten gains.

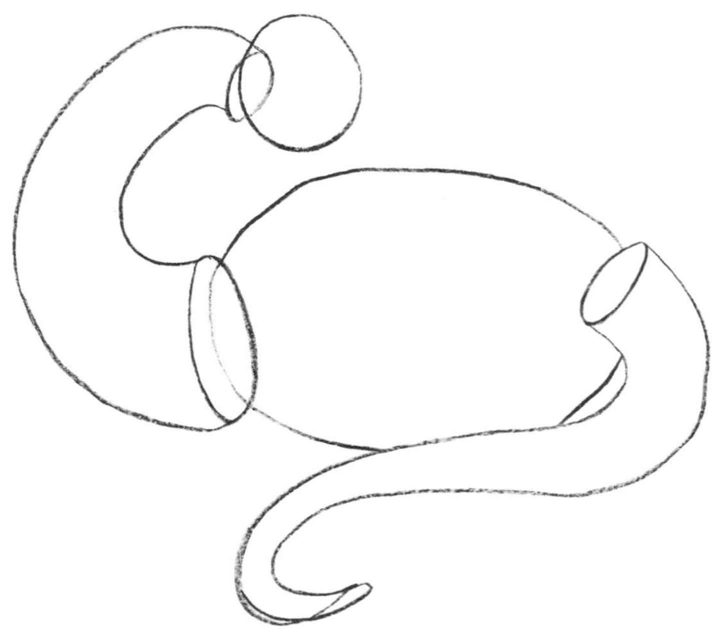

Step One I start this drake by mapping out the form of the creature's body. I use a harder pencil—a 2H—because I know most of this information is for me and will soon fall victim to the eraser.

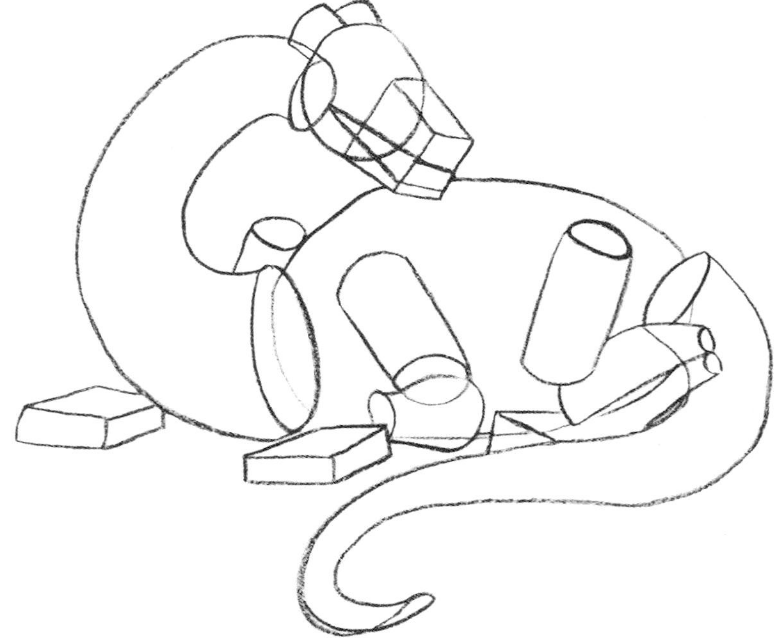

Step Two After adding a boxlike snout and the back of the head, I block in the legs and feet using boxes and cylinders.

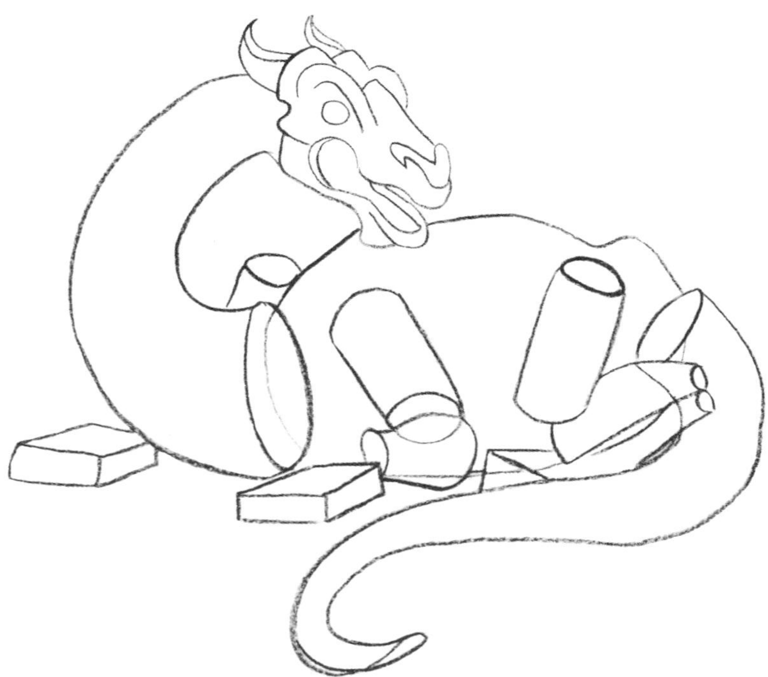

Step Three Following the form I laid out, I use an HB pencil to develop the head, which is similar to a horse's skull. The nose resembles a llama's. Next I modify the shape of the lower body by drawing a bony ridge near the tail.

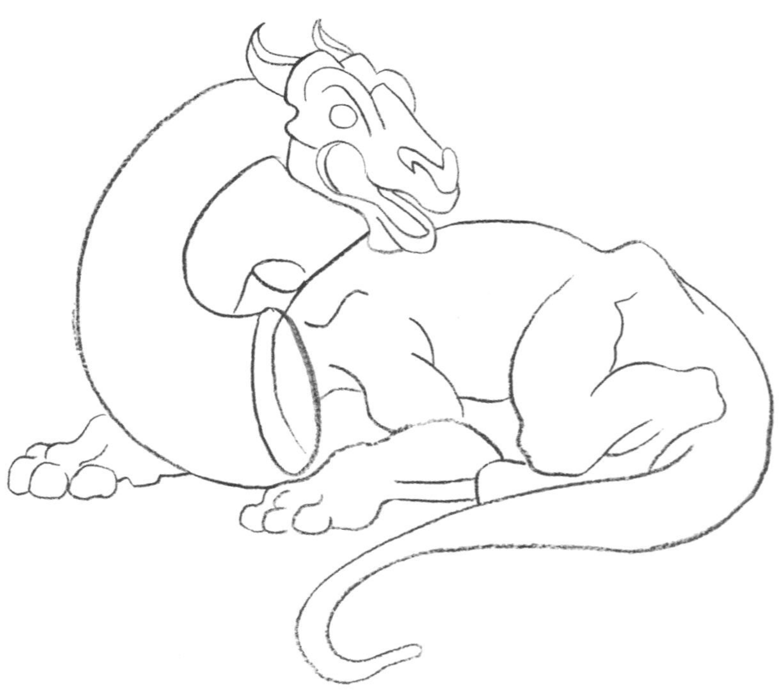

Step Four I integrate the tail into the body and develop the legs, using my basic shapes as guides. I refine the feet, making the toes appear lumpy and oversized. Before erasing my construction lines, I modify the end of the tail by thinning it out a bit.

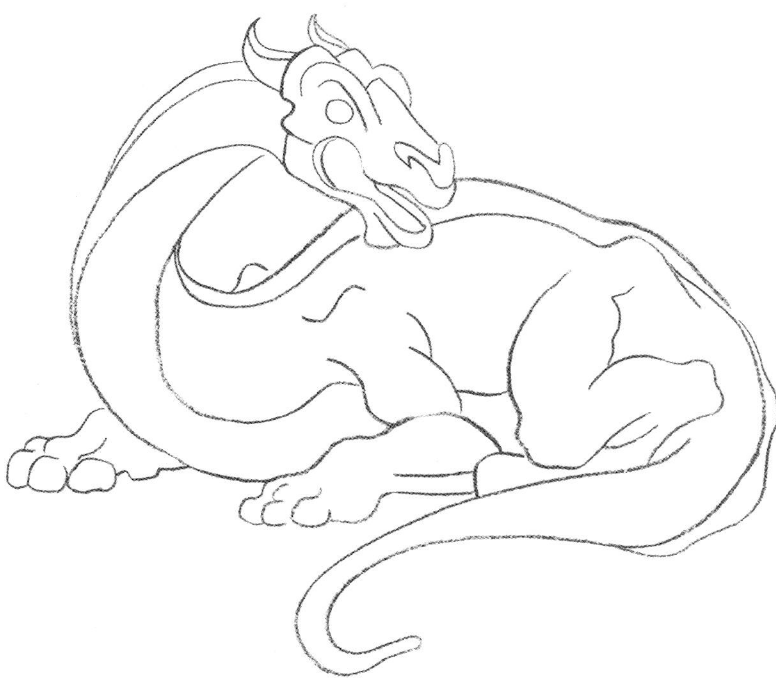

Step Five To give form to the neck, I add curved lines to represent the underside and top sections. I also draw a stripe that goes from the base of the neck to the middle of the tail to show the ridge of the back, and I refine the shoulder that is visible on the far side of the dragon's body.

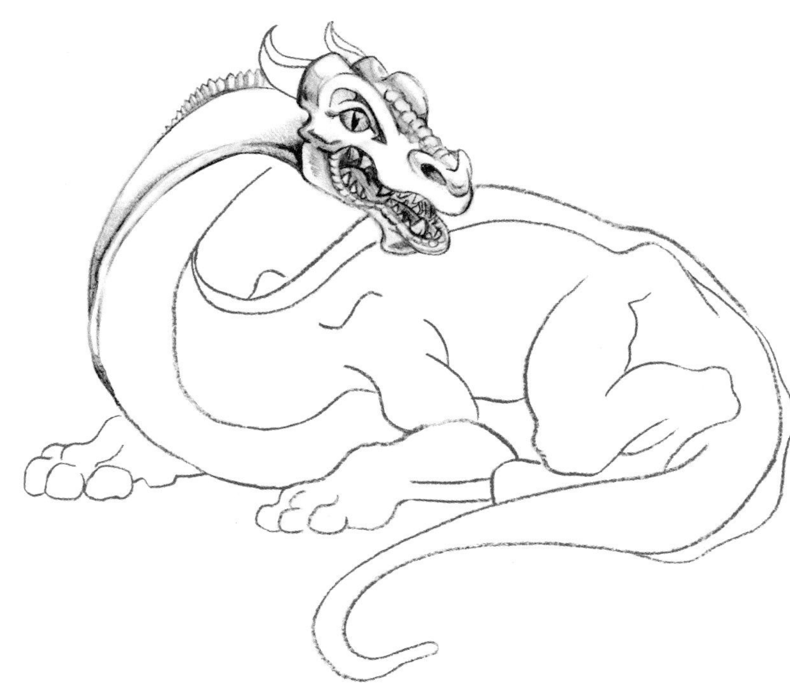

Step Six I want to give this dragon a fierce personality, so I use my 2B pencil to add the sharp, jagged teeth and the small, bony plates along the back of the neck. I also detail the eye and add a ridged texture to the nose. Then I add tone to the base of the horns, the nose, inside the mouth, and along the side of the neck. The darkest values are inside the mouth and at the top of the neck, where the jaw bone casts a shadow.

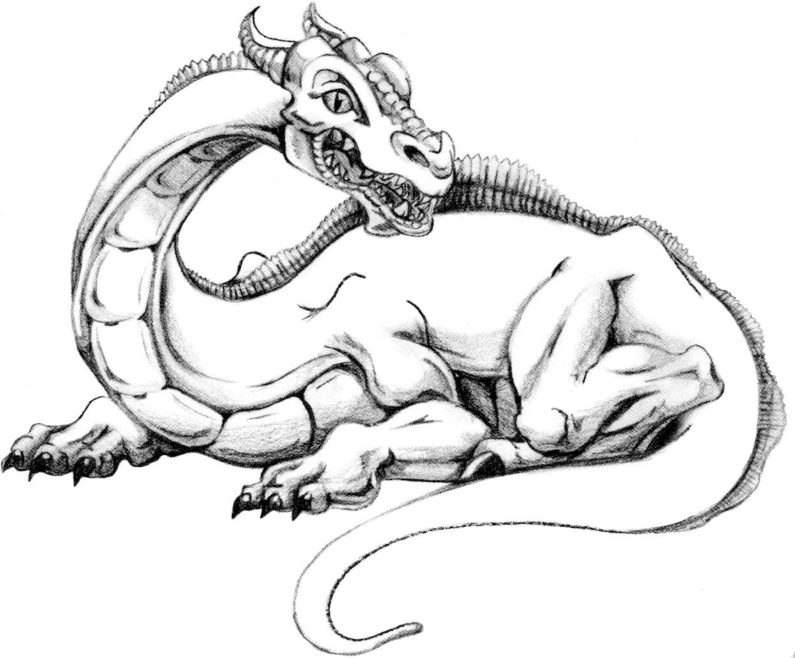

Step Seven I continue drawing bony plates along the ridge of the back, making them taller and sharper near the middle of the back. Then I add large scales on the underside of the neck and belly. I apply dark tone where the head casts a shadow onto the neck. And I add tone to the legs, creating a darker value where the body parts overlap. I shade the feet, drawing long, dark claws with a highlight on each toe. I also begin to draw ridges on the horns.

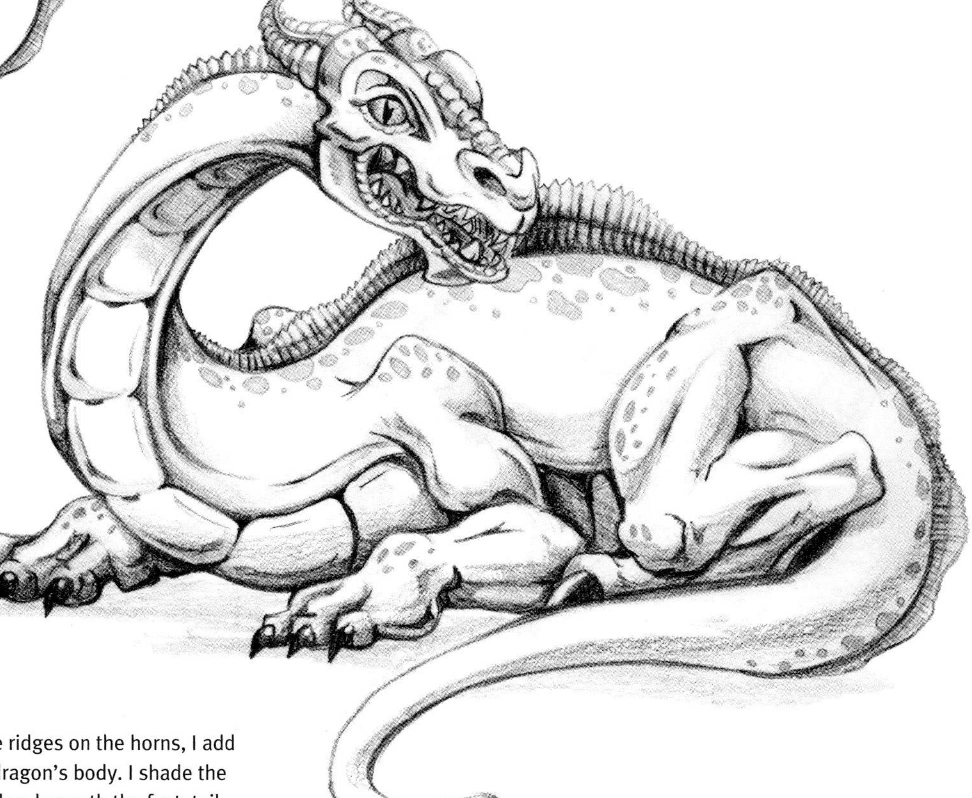

Step Eight After I finish the ridges on the horns, I add irregular spots all over the dragon's body. I shade the dragon's tail and add a shadow beneath the feet, tail, and torso to "ground" the beast into the scene.

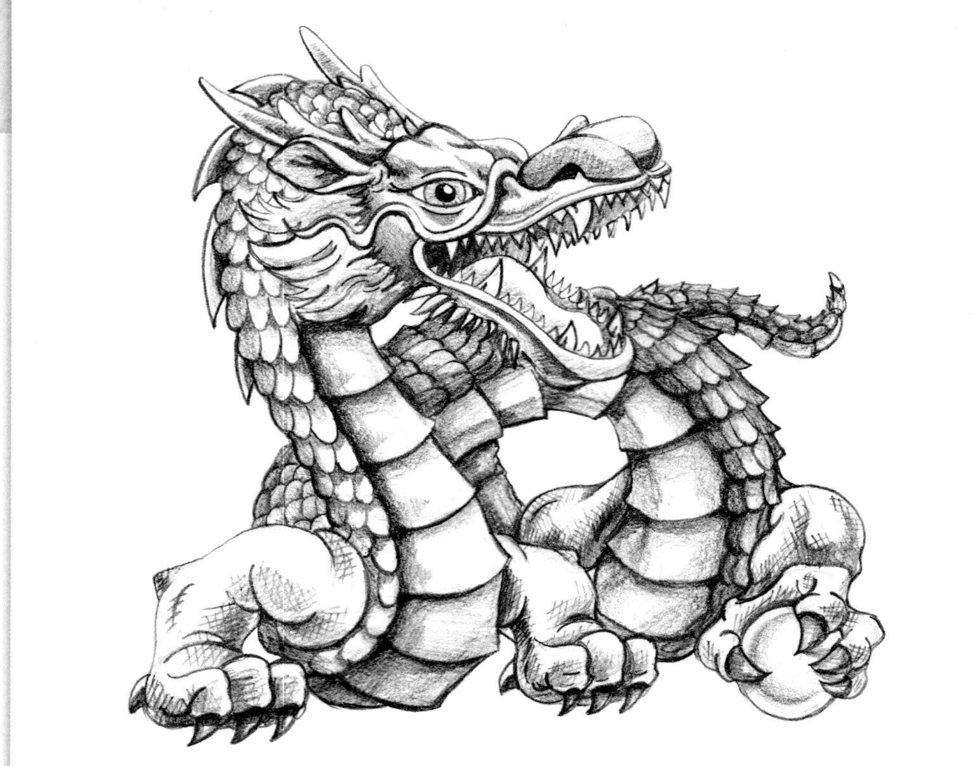

About the Artist

Michael Dobrzycki is an accomplished painter, carpenter, puppet maker, and sketch artist whose work has been featured in more than a dozen children's books and small press publications over the last few years. Michael's illustration career began in 1999, when he toured the United States performing a one-man sketch-artist show called "Disney Doodles." Soon after, he began illustrating children's books for Yakovetic Productions. Michael has been a featured artist on Disney Channel Australia, and he was inducted into the Disneyland Entertainment Hall of Fame in 2001. Michael received his MFA in illustration from the California State University, Fullerton, and holds a BA in both art and history from Whittier College, where he has taught as a visiting professor. Michael currently serves on the Whittier Cultural Arts Foundation's Board of Directors.